AMERICAN APPETITES

FOOD AND FOODWAYS

SERIES EDITOR:
JENNIFER JENSEN WALLACH

American Appetites

A DOCUMENTARY READER

EDITED BY
JENNIFER JENSEN WALLACH
AND LINDSEY R. SWINDALL

The University of Arkansas Press
Fayetteville
2014

ISBN: 978-1-55728-668-0
eISBN: 978-1-61075-550-4

18   17   16   15   14   5   4   3   2   1

Designed by Liz Lester

⊗ The paper used in this publication meets the minimum requirements
of the American National Standard for Permanence of Paper for Printed
Library Materials Z39.48–1984.

Library of Congress Control Number: 2014934712

This project was supported in part by the
Julia Child Foundation for Gastronomy and the Culinary Arts.

COVER IMAGE: The Faro Caudill family eating dinner in their dugout, Pie Town,
New Mexico. Photograph by Russell Lee, 1940. Farm Security Administration/Office
of War Information Color Photographs, Library of Congress, LC-DIG-fsac-1a34105.

COVER DESIGN: Liz Lester

For our fathers,

Marshall G. Swindall,
who taught me to love both cooking and history,

and David A. Jensen, who read to me

CONTENTS

SERIES EDITOR'S PREFACE

The University of Arkansas Press series Food and Foodways explores historical and contemporary issues in global food studies. We are committed to telling lesser-known food stories and to representing a diverse set of voices. Our strength is works in the humanities and social sciences that use food as a lens to examine broader social, cultural, environmental, ethical, and economic issues. However, we recognize that food—perhaps the most central of all human concerns—is not only a barometer by which to gauge social, cultural, and environmental conditions but can also be a source of pleasure. In addition to scholarly books, we publish creative nonfiction that explores the sensory dimensions of consumption and celebrates food as evidence of human creativity and innovation.

The first title in the series, *American Appetites: A Documentary Reader,* edited by myself and Lindsey R. Swindall, is indicative of our desire to document a multiplicity of food stories. This documentary reader is the first to engage the entire span of US food history, from the time before European contact through the present. It captures a range of voices—victims of conquest and triumphant imperialists, gluttons and abstainers, those who prepare food and those who are served. Collectively these documents reveal that although Americans have generally enjoyed food abundance not everyone has had equal access to the communal table. *American Appetites* documents more than the material aspects of our food culture, giving insights into what Americans have eaten, telling us who received more than their share and who went hungry. It also demonstrates that foodways can be decoded to reveal much about our cultural values and anxieties.

American Appetites demonstrates that the quest for nourishment has always been about far more than survival. Food habits reveal a great deal about our aspirations, our flaws, and our human potential. Readers of *American Appetites* will discover that an understanding of the country's food history does not merely add an ornamental layer to our grasp of the nation's history. Our national cravings for food are deeply intertwined with a story of conquest and avarice, of retrenchment and reversals, a painful past that we doggedly hope might lead us toward a more equitable future.

JENNIFER JENSEN WALLACH

ACKNOWLEDGMENTS

We are grateful to *The Nation* magazine for allowing us to republish "Waiters and Waitresses" from the December 10, 1874, issue. James McWilliams and A. Breeze Harper also generously allowed us to publish excerpts from their food studies blogs in the final chapter. F. Todd Smith and Kelly Wisecup offered valuable scholarly advice and suggestions, and Charles Bittner, as always, offered indefatigable research assistance. Erin Dorris Cassidy, associate professor in the Newton Gresham Library, was a great help in replying to research queries promptly. Lindsey would like to gratefully recognize her mother, Lizabeth Foster, who kindly supplied the recipes from her grandmother, Bonnie Sealey, as well as Robert Blake Tritico and Frank E. Tritico Jr., who shared the photo and stories of their family's grocery store in Houston. We are grateful to have had the opportunity to work with the excellent staff at the University of Arkansas Press, including David Scott Cunningham, Melissa King, and Tyler Lail. The new director of the press, Mike Bieker, enthusiastically supported our vision for the book as we completed this volume. We appreciate and recognize his interest in advancing the field of food studies. Copy editor Karen Johnson's work was invaluable, aiding us in making sure we got the details right. Our warmest thanks go out to Julie Watkins and Larry Malley, the founders of the University of Arkansas Press series Food and Foodways. Their warmth, humor, and vision are unparalleled.

INTRODUCTION

In his ambitious global history, *Near a Thousand Tables: A History of Food*, Felipe Fernández-Armesto convincingly argues, "Food has a claim to be considered the world's most important subject. It is what matters most to most people for most of the time."[1] Despite this perceptive and seemingly non-controversial observation, food has typically not been considered a fitting subject for historical inquiry. The practices of preparing and consuming food have often been taken for granted, as an obvious but not particularly revealing backdrop to all other human behavior. Issues like hunger and food production have often been invoked, for example, as explanations for civil unrest or as illustrations of advancements in technology. However, more often than not, topics such as these have been raised only in passing, worthy of mention but not of extensive contemplation. Professional historians have almost completely ignored daily eating practices such as decisions about what to eat and with whom until the recent advent of food history, a field that is beginning to show signs of maturation in the twenty-first century.[2]

When historical study was professionalized first in Germany and later elsewhere in Europe and in the United Sates in the late nineteenth century, students of the discipline interpreted their task as that of documenting the machinations of politicians and the tactics and outcomes of military conflicts. Not only was their focus almost solely upon the political arena and upon nation building, but practitioners of this newly legitimated profession also saw themselves as scientists who were able to compile singular and irrefutable truths about a complex, multifaceted past. Decade by decade, this vision of what it means to study the past has expanded, and by the middle of the twentieth century the field had been reinvigorated by a "new social history," which provided a much needed counterpoint to the "great men" histories of the past. Professional historians were newly empowered to ask different questions and to expand their areas of inquiry to include the study of ordinary people.

New social historians endeavored to understand topics such as the formation of social classes and movements and processes such as industrialization and urbanization. The new social history bore the imprint of the social reform movements of the second half of the twentieth century as well, and social historians began to emphasize the diversity of human experience and to tell the stories of members of minority groups, women, and the working classes. Initially, however, this new drive to document the diverse experiences of the non-elite was still fueled by the belief in the possibility of objectivity, and some new social historians were strongly influenced by the quantitative methods employed by social scientists. Studies of this ilk might document the consumption patterns of ordinary people but often neglected to analyze the personal and social significance of dietary decisions.

Increasingly, however, different epistemological assumptions became embedded in this new, more democratic history, and a cultural turn moved social history away from the positivism that had characterized history from the time of its professionalization. Truth was now construed as being at least somewhat perspectival, and the statistical models of the social scientist were increasingly complicated by an analysis of things that cannot easily be quantified. Historians who were influenced by social anthropologists and literary critics paid more attention to topics such as the art, popular culture, literature, manners, leisure activities, and various customs of a given society. It was the turn to culture that helped pave the way for serious historical treatises about the meaning of food.[3]

Cultural histories serve as important reminders about how a study of foodways can illuminate all fields of historical inquiry. Not only does food history yield clues that are of use to social and cultural historians who aim to resuscitate forgotten histories of everyday people, but the study of food also has the potential to reinvigorate historical questions about power struggles in the realms of politics and the battleground that animated the first generation of professional historians. The search for food is a powerful motivator in some military skirmishes, and its scarcity is a determining factor in the outcome of others. Just as Jefferson Davis had to respond to the women who rioted for bread during the Civil War, all politicians must answer to hungry citizens whose anger might threaten their grasp on power. Eating can also be a performance on the campaign trail of a democratic country as vote seekers consume local foods as a means of demonstrating grassroots solidarity. Even those historians who have shied away from the sometimes slippery task of cultural analysis in favor of the quantifiable have much to gain from the study of food. Data about prices, quantity, and the types of food produced and consumed can reveal much about the health—economic and otherwise—of a nation.

Scholars working in the field of United States history have capitalized on this culinary turn and have used foodways as a lens to reexamine a variety of familiar subjects. For example, historians James McWilliams and Trudy Eden have looked at how food practices reflected and also helped shape the creation of a uniquely American identity.[4] Eden's study yields insights into early modern ideas about nutrition, which included an almost literal understanding of the cliché "you are what you eat," and McWilliams examines the process of what he calls the "culinary declaration of independence" that occurred when emancipated British colonials learned to reimagine their foodways as being those of a republican nation. In her seminal study *Hungering for America: Italian, Irish, and Jewish Foodways in the Age of Migration*, Hasia Diner fast-forwards the analysis of food identity construction in the United States to the nineteenth century in her examination of how immigrants used food habits to define their relationship both to their countries of origin and to their newly adopted home, often by modifying their cuisine to incorporate aspects of the table associated with both geographies.[5] Laura Shapiro and Megan Elias have explored the role that food has played in constructing ideas about gender, and Psyche Williams-Forson has showed how illuminating food studies can be in deciphering the peculiarities of racial thinking in the United States.[6] More recently, US historians have used food habits as a way to examine the construction of scientific knowledge. For example, in *Eating Right in America: The Cultural Politics of Food and Health*, Charlotte Biltekoff has urged historians to look for moral messages embedded in allegedly neutral scientific advice about nutrition.[7]

The titles mentioned here merely scratch the surface of a rapidly proliferating and intellectually exciting field that tests existing assumptions about issues ranging from the dynamics of colonization to the creation and recreation of ideas about race and gender to the construction of categories of knowledge. The "For Further Reading" section at the end of this book provides interested readers with a bibliography that will direct them to other texts that collectively challenge students of US history not to take issues of food production and consumption for granted.

Predicated on the belief that the study of foodways can shed light on a variety of issues in US political, economic, social, and cultural history, *American Appetites* contains food-related primary sources, which are encapsulated in contextual headnotes. Pioneering food historian Jeffrey Pilcher argues, "Although professional historians were slow to perceive the importance of food, the evidence was always there waiting in primary sources."[8] This rich assortment of firsthand evidence—ranging from folktales to cookbooks to slave narratives to government propaganda—demonstrates the truth of Pilcher's claim. The documents and images assembled here aim to guide the reader on a journey through US history that is focused on the nation's collective stomach. Eating is a prelude to all other aspects of human behavior, and there is no more fundamental starting point for examining the American experience than at the metaphorical table.

The eleven chapters of *American Appetites* begin the chronicle of American food habits in the pre-Columbian era and end with the present day, demonstrating that an examination of foodways has much to teach students of the American past. Readers can chart fluctuating ideas of what it means to be an American through the changing consumption patterns of those who inhabited the geographical space of what became the United States. For example, through the testimony of European explorers and Native American foundational myths, which are reprinted here, *American Appetites* documents foundational American foods as well as the transformation of the American palate. Accounts of the rations served on the Middle Passage of the transatlantic slave trade and firsthand testimony about the food eaten by those in bondage reveal that slavery in the United States can also be freshly examined through the lens of food habits. Newspaper stories, which are excerpted here, express wonderment about the unfamiliar foodways of immigrants who arrived to the United States in the late nineteenth and early twentieth centuries. When these are read in conjunction with a xenophobic ditty about the taste sensibilities of a Chinese immigrant, readers will gain a sense of the complexity of American attitudes toward the incorporation of new residents. Excerpts from memoirs and oral histories of homesteaders and migrant workers demonstrate how food was a powerful force propelling internal movement such as western expansion. The primary sources compiled here also reveal that eating practices can reflect shared religious values, patriotic fervor, and aesthetic sensibilities. For example, devout Seventh-Day Adventist John Harvey Kellogg offered advice for a bland diet that he believed would promote female chastity, while T. D. Duncan's 1878 handbook *How to Be Plump* encouraged prodigious consumption as a beauty secret. Dietary beliefs give clues about contemporary scientific understanding and varying philosophies about how resources should be distributed. These issues are captured in documents that record the evolving nutritional advice issued by the US Department of Agriculture and in a pamphlet justifying federal food assistance for the needy. Also reprinted here are food histories that give insights into the importance of food during times of military conflict; these range from a letter written by a Civil War solider expressing gratitude for a food parcel from home to government propaganda urging food conservation during both World War I and World War II. The food histories invoked in this volume capture the histories of a diverse group of people: the rich and the poor, the powerful and the powerless, the hungry and the sated, and everyone in between.

NOTES

1. Felipe Fernández-Armesto, *Near a Thousand Tables: A History of Food* (New York: Simon Schuster, 2001), ix.

2. Many independent scholars who self-identify as "culinary historians" have long been interested in issues such as recipes and cooking techniques. In contrast, academics working in the new field of "food history" use food as a lens to examine a wide range of social and cultural issues. For an analysis of the distinction between these two fields, see "Culinary History vs. Food History," by Barbara Haber, in *The Oxford Handbook to American Food and Drink, ed.* Andrew F. Smith (Oxford: Oxford University Press, 2007), 179–80.

3. See Jeffrey Pilcher, "Cultural Histories of Food," in *The Oxford Handbook of Food History, ed. Jeffery Pilcher* (Oxford: Oxford University Press, 2012), 41–60.

4. Trudy Eden, *The Early American Table: Food and Society in the New World* (Dekalb: Northern Illinois University Press, 2008); James McWilliams, *A Revolution in Eating: How the Quest for Food Shaped America* (New York: Columbia University Press, 2005).

5. Hasia Diner, *Hungering for America: Italian, Irish, and Jewish Foodways in the Age of Migration* (Cambridge: Harvard University Press, 2003).

6. Laura Shapiro, *Perfection Salad: Women and Cooking at the Turn of the Twentieth Century* (Berkeley: University of California Press, 1986); Megan Elias, *Stir It Up: Home Economics in American Culture* (Philadelphia: University of Pennsylvania Press, 2008); Psyche Williams-Forson, *Building Houses out of Chicken Legs: Black Women, Food, and Power* (Chapel Hill: University of North Carolina Press, 2006).

7. Charlotte Biltekoff, *Eating Right in America: The Cultural Politics of Food and Health* (Durham: Duke University Press, 2013).

8. Jeffrey Pilcher, introduction to *The Oxford Handbook of Food History*, ed. Pilcher, xvii.

AMERICAN APPETITES

CHAPTER 1

Foundational Food

The cuisine of the contemporary United States is an outgrowth of a history of colonization, conquest, and migration. It is the result of the transfer and combination of culinary knowledge and ingredients from throughout the globe. The origins of the eclectic American style of eating are the food habits of various groups of Native Americans who first learned how to transform indigenous plants and animals into food and passed this information along to the outsiders who encroached on their terrain beginning in the fifteenth century.

At the time of European contact, specific native food habits varied due to geography and to cultural preferences. For example, tribes residing on the Northwest coast adopted fish, especially salmon, as a culinary staple. Those living in the Great Plains turned to bison for their major source of dietary protein. Many Native Americans were farmers who supplemented their diets through hunting and gathering. Those who focused more on hunting often traded with other tribes, exchanging game for agricultural products. Maize, a form of wild grass that was domesticated in Mexico 7,000 years ago and gradually spread northward, reached what is now the southwestern United States approximately 3,200 years ago. The plant was a key food for many indigenous people and was destined to become a staple for the foreigners who invaded or were transported to the continent as well. The precontact American larder contained a wide variety of wild fruit, greens, and nuts; cultivated squash and beans; and game such as deer and turkey.

The documents in this chapter give glimpses of the variegated and complex cuisine of the Amerindians, both from the perspective of folklore and from the observations of European arrivals who regarded the diets of the local people they met with responses ranging from curiosity to horror to envy. Regardless of their initial response, the foodways they encountered were foundational in establishing a unique and enduring American way of eating.

DOCUMENT 1:

The Arapaho Learn How to Hunt Buffalo

Source: "The Origins of Culture," in George A. Dorsey and Alfred L. Kroeber, *Traditions of the Arapaho* (Chicago: Field Columbian Museum, 1903), 7–8.

The Arapaho originally lived in the eastern plains in present-day Colorado and Wyoming. This myth seeks to explain how they originally learned to hunt American bison, often referred to as "buffalo." The animal not only was once their primary food source, but also was utilized to make items like clothing and tipis. This story reveals how central the bison were to their culture and collective sense of identity. This way of life was disrupted ultimately in the late nineteenth century when the Arapaho relocated to reservations in Oklahoma and Wyoming and the bison became scarce due to a variety of factors, including overhunting by non-indigenous people and eradication schemes.

A man tried to think how the people might kill buffalo. He was a hard thinker. He would go off for several days and fast. He did this repeatedly. At last he dreamed that a voice spoke to him and told him what to do. He went back to the people and made an inclosure of trees set in the ground with willows wound between them. At one side of the inclosure, however, there was only a cliff with rocks at the bottom. Then four untiring runners were sent out to the windward of a herd of buffalo, two of them on each side. They headed the buffalo and drove them toward the inclosure and into it. Then the buffalo were run about inside until a heavy cloud of dust rose and in this, unable to see, they ran over the precipice and were killed.

This man also procured horses for the people. There were many wild horses. The man had an inclosure made which was complete except for an opening. Horses were driven into this just as the buffalo had been, and then the opening was closed. The horses ran around until they were tired; then they were lassoed. At first it took a long time to break them. In the beginning only one horse was caught for each family, but this was not enough and more were caught. After a few years the horses bred, and soon every man had a herd. The dogs now no longer had to drag the meat and baggage, nor did the women have to carry part on their backs.

The people had nothing to cut up meat with. A man took a buffalo shoulder blade and with flint cut out a narrow piece of it. He sharpened it, and thus had a knife. Then he also made a knife from flint by flaking it into shape. All the people learned how to make knives.

This man also made the first bow and arrows. He made the arrow point of the short rib of a buffalo. Having made a bow and four arrows, he went off alone and waited in the timber at a buffalo path. A buffalo came and he shot: the arrow disappeared into the body and the animal fell dead. Then he killed three more. He went back and told the people: "Harness the dogs; there are four dead buffalo in the timber." So from this time the people were able to get meat without driving the buffalo into an inclosure.

The people used the fire drill. A man went off alone and fasted. He learned that certain stones, when struck, would give a spark and that this spark would light tinder. He gathered stones and filled a small horn with soft, dry wood. Then he went home. His wife said to him: "Please make a fire." He took out his horn and his flint stones, struck a spark, blew it, put grass on, and soon, to the astonishment of all who saw it, had a fire. This was much easier than using the fire drill, and the people soon all did it.

These three men who procured the buffalo inclosure and the horses, the knife and the bow, and fire, were the ones who brought the people to the condition in which they live.

The Iroquois Learn to Grow Beans, Corn, and Squash Together

Source: "Corn Plume and Bean Maiden,"
in Mabel Powers, *Stories Iroquois Tell Their Children* (New York: American Book Company, 1917), 180–86.

For the Iroquois of the northeastern region of what is now the United States, cultivated corn, beans, and squash have always been central items in their cuisine. They have often referred to these food items as the "Three Sisters." This myth offers one explanation for why this group of Amerindians has traditionally grown these three crops in close proximity to each other. This version of the story was recorded by Mabel Powers, a European American who studied Iroquois culture and published several books on the subject. In 1910 she was adopted by the Tonawanda Seneca Nation, and the people gave her the name Yeshenhwehs, which means "she who carries and tells the stories."

The Great Spirit had smiled upon his Red Children. The land was filled with plenty, for the Great Spirit had given to them the three sustainers of life, the corn, the bean, and the squash. Flowers bloomed, birds sang, and all the earth was glad with the Red Children, for the gifts of the Great Spirit.

On one side of a hill grew the tall, waving corn, with its silk tassels and plumes. On another side, beans, with their velvety pods, climbed toward the sky. Some distance down a third slope, beautiful yellow squashes turned their faces to the sun.

One day, the Spirit of the corn grew restless. There came a rustling through the waving leaves, and a great sigh burst from the heart of the tall stalks. The Spirit of the corn was lonely.

After that, every morning at sunrise, a handsome young chief was seen to come and stand on the brow of the hill. On his head were shining red plumes. Tall, and strong, and splendid he stood, wrapped in the folds of his waving blanket, whose fringed tassels danced to the summer breeze.

"Che che hen! Che che hen! Some one I would marry! Some one I would marry!" the young chieftain would sing, many, many times.

One day, his voice reached the Squash Maiden, on the other side of the hill. The Squash Maiden drew about her a rich green blanket, into which she had woven many flaunting gold trumpet-shaped flowers. Then she ran swiftly to the young chieftain.

"Marry me! Marry me!" said the Squash Maiden, as she spread her beautiful gold and green blanket at his feet.

Corn Plume looked down at the Squash Maiden sitting on her blanket at his feet. She was good to look upon, and yet Corn Plume was not content. He wanted a maiden who would stand by his side, not always sit at his feet.

Then Corn Plume spoke thus to the Squash Maiden.

"Corn Plume cannot marry Squash Maiden. She is very beautiful, but she will not make song in Corn Plume's heart. Squash Maiden will grow tired of his lodge. She will not stay in his wigwam. She likes to go a long trail, and wander far from the lodge."

"Corn Plume cannot make Squash Maiden his wife, for he is not content with her. But she shall be Corn Plume's sister, and sit in his lodge whenever she will. The maiden Corn Plume weds must be ever at his side. She must go where he goes, stay where he stays."

Next morning at sunrise, the voice of Corn Plume was again heard, singing from the hilltop, "Che che hen! Che che hen! Some one I would marry! Some one I would marry! Che che hen! Che che hen!"

This time his song reached the ears of the Bean Maiden. Her heart sang, when she heard the voice of Corn Plume, for she knew that he was calling her. So light of heart was Bean Maiden, that she ran like a deer up the hillside. On and on, up and over the brow of the hill she climbed, till she reached the young chieftain's side.

Then Corn Plume turned and beheld the most beautiful maiden he had ever seen. Her eyes were deep and dark, like mountain pools. Her breath was sweet as the waters of the maple. She threw off her blanket of green, and purple, and white, and stretched her twining arms to him.

Corn Plume desired to keep Bean Maiden forever close to him. He bent his tall plumed head to her. Her arms wound round and round the young chieftain, and Corn Plume was content.

So closely were the arms of Corn Plume and the Bean Maiden entwined, so truly were they wed, that the Indians never attempted to separate them. Ever after, corn and beans were planted in the same hill, and often a squash seed was added.

Since the Great Spirit had placed the corn, the bean, and the squash together on a hill, the Indian said they should continue to live and grow and occupy a hill together.

The door of Corn Plume's lodge was ever open to the Squash Maiden, if she chose to enter. But seldom did she stay in his wigwam. More often, she was found running off on a long trail.

But Bean Maiden remained true to Corn Plume. Always she was found by his side. Never did she leave the lodge unless he went with her. Corn Plume's lodge was her lodge, and her trail was his trail.

And because the Spirits of the corn and the bean are as one, the Indians not only plant and grow them together, but cook and eat them together.

"In life, they were one," they say, "We will not separate them in death."

And now, when a great rustling and sighing of the corn is heard in the White man's land, the Indians often say, "'Tis the Spirit of Corn Plume, crying for his lost Bean Maiden!"

DOCUMENT 3:

Spanish Explorer Francisco Vásquez de Coronado Encounters Pueblo Food, 1540

Source: George Parker Winship, ed. and trans., *The Coronado Expedition, 1540–1542* (Washington, DC: Government Printing Office, 1896), 559–60.

In 1540, Spanish explorer Francisco Vásquez de Coronado led an expedition of three hundred Spanish soldiers and approximately one thousand Indians on a journey throughout the Southwest in a search for the legendary golden cities of Cibola. They did not find the vast stores of wealth they hoped for and clashed violently with local Native Americans. Coronado's notes from his expedition give some insights into the food habits of the contemporary Pueblo peoples, whose diet was built around the staple of maize.

The food which they eat in this country is corn, of which they have a great abundance, & beans & venison, which they probably eat (although they say that they do not), because we found many skins of deer and hares and rabbits. They make the best corn cakes I have ever seen anywhere, and this is what everybody ordinarily eats. They have the very best arrangement and machinery for grinding that was ever seen. One of these Indian women here will grind as much as four of the Mexicans. They have very good salt in crystals, which they bring from a lake a day's journey distant from here. No information can be obtained among them about the North Sea or that on the west, nor do I know how to tell Your Lordship which we are nearest to. I should judge that it is nearer to the western, and 150 leagues is the nearest that it seems to me it can be thither. The North Sea ought to be much farther away. Your Lordship may thus see how very wide the country is. They have many animals—bears, tigers, lions, porcupines, and some sheep as big as a horse, with very large horns and little tails. I have seen some of their horns the size of which was something to marvel at. There are also wild goats, whose heads I have seen, and the paws of the bears and the skins of the wild boars. For game they have deer, leopards, & very large deer.

DOCUMENT 4:

Athanase de Mézières Describes Wichita Food Habits in Eighteenth-Century Texas

Source: Howard Eugene Bolton, ed. and trans., *Athanase De Mezieres and the Louisiana Texas*

Frontier, 1768–1780 (Cleveland: Arthur H. Curk, 1914), 203–4.

Athanase de Mézières was a Frenchman who began a military career in Louisiana in the 1730s. After the region passed from French to Spanish control in 1763, he became a Spanish diplomat to the Native Americans and the lieutenant governor of Natchitoches. In the course of his duties he traveled widely and recorded his impressions of the culture of the people he encountered, including the foodways of the Wichita living near the Red River.

Señor Commandant-General, My dear Sir: The nation of the Taovayazes is divided into two villages, one situated on the northern bank of the Vermejo, or Natchitoches River, the other opposite the first on the other bank. The former is composed of thirty-seven houses, the latter of one hundred twenty-three.... Their dress, consisting only of shirts, leggins, and moccasins, is of skins; their leather shields, horse equipment, and camping tents are of the same material. Their foresight in supplying provisions shows them to be industrious, for there is no house in which at present there may not be seen four or five vessels full of maize, each one estimated at four and a half *fanegas* besides a great quantity of beans and calabashes. They preserve the latter from year to year, weaving them curiously like mats. In addition, they raise watermelons and tobacco in great plenty. The abundance of the springs furnishes them fresh and crystalline water to drink, moistens and fertilizes the broad plains where they plant their crops, and offers itself to any one who may wish to irrigate them. That of the river, which is healthful, is a perpetual snare for the cattle that are always in sight, and which they kill at all times. The fish are of the best varieties, but they do not care for them. They have fire-wood right at hand, securing it from that Grand Forest of which I have spoken. This is eighty leagues long, and from one to two wide, and even more in parts, and in it bear and wild boars are found. Nor is there any scarcity of useful timber, such as poplar, ash, elm, and black and white walnut, the former valuable for lumber, the latter to supply oil. The quarries seem to challenge use, but they serve the Indians only for whetstones to sharpen their hatchets, grinding stones to make *mutates*, white stones for lances, and flint stones to tip their arrows and to make fire. The temperature is neither too hot nor too cold. Finally, in order that they may lack nothing that is necessary, they are provided with a bank of excellent salt in the middle of the river, which is formed there in such a way that, when a part has been removed, the loss is restored in a short while, just as if it were made anew—a most wonderful product, a sample of which I have the honor to send to your Lordship, as it seems to me worthy of your attention. . . .

Their government is democratic, not even excluding the women, in consideration of what they contribute to the welfare of the republic. The women tan, sew, and paint the skins, fence in the fields, care for the cornfields, harvest the crops, cut and fetch the fire-wood, prepare the food, build the houses, and rear the children, their constant care stopping at nothing that contributes to the comfort and pleasure of their husbands. The latter devote themselves wholly to the chase and to warfare. By the first they become rich, by the second famous. They come to be petty chiefs among their people, not by the prowess of their fathers, but by their own. To this is added the thought that in proportion to their achievements they will gain for themselves happiness in the next life. They have no religion, or very little, the most noticeable feature of it being the veneration of fire, together with ridiculous superstitions. They are cheerful, affable, and docile in their manner, compassionate toward the sick, orphans, and widows, respectful to their elders, generous toward strangers, kind to guests, but in general more revengeful for injury than grateful for benefits, as is proved by the atrocities which their prisoners experience at their hands, which are so great that even to relate them would cause horror and make the narrator a party to them. . . .

May God preserve your Lordship many years. Taovayazes, April 18, 1778.

I kiss the hand of your Lordship, etc.

Atanasio de Mezieres.

DOCUMENT 5:

Antoine-Simon Le Page du Pratz Describes the Food of Eighteenth-Century Louisiana

Source: Antoine-Simon Le Page du Pratz,
*History of Louisiana or of The Western Parts
Of Virginia And Carolina* (1774).

Frenchman Antoine-Simon Le Page du Pratz arrived in Louisiana in 1718. He established a plantation near present-day Natchez, Mississippi, where he grew tobacco, exploiting the labor of enslaved Africans and an enslaved Chitimacha woman. Le Page du Pratz traveled widely in the area, often guided by local Natchez Indians, whose language he learned. He recorded detailed observations about the local flora and fauna. In this passage he describes how maize and other local crops were cultivated and consumed by the Natchez. He also gives insights into the culinary transformation taking place during this period with his description of the cultivation of food crops such as wheat and rice, which were introduced into the region by Europeans.

During my abode in that country, where I myself have a grant of lands, and where I lived sixteen years, I have had leisure to study this subject. . . . The reader may depend upon my being faithful and exact; he must not however here expect a description of every thing that Louisiana produces of the vegetable kind. Its prodigious fertility makes it impracticable for me to undertake so extensive a work. I shall chiefly describe those plants and fruits that are most useful to the inhabitants, either in regard to their own subsistence or preservation, or in regard to their foreign commerce; and I shall add the manner of cultivating and managing the plants that are of greatest advantage to the colony.

Louisiana produces several kinds of Maiz, namely Flour-maiz, which is white, with a flat and shrivelled surface, and is the softest of all the kinds; Homony corn, which is round, hard, and shining; of this there are four sorts, the white, the yellow, the red, and the blue; the Maiz of these two last colours is more common in the high lands than in the Lower Louisiana. We have besides small corn, or small Maiz, so called because it is smaller than the other kinds. New settlers sow this corn upon their first arrival, in order to have whereon to subsist as soon as possible; for it rises very fast, and ripens in so short a time, that from the same field they may have two crops of it in one year. Besides this, it has the advantage of being more agreeable to the taste than the large kind.

Maiz, which in France is called Turkey Corn, (and in England Indian Corn) is the natural product of this country; for upon our arrival we found it cultivated by the natives. It grows upon a stalk six, seven, and eight feet high; the ear is large, and about two inches diameter, containing sometimes seven hundred grains and upwards; and each stalk bears sometimes six or seven ears, according to the goodness of the ground. The black and light soil is that which agrees best with it; but strong ground is not so favourable to it.

This corn, it is well known, is very wholesome both for man and other animals, especially for poultry. The natives, that they may have change of dishes, dress it in various ways. The best is to make it into what is called Parched Meal, (Farine Froide.) As there is nobody who does not eat of this with pleasure, even though not very hungry, I will give the manner of preparing it, that our provinces of France, which reap this grain, may draw the same advantage from it.

The corn is first parboiled in water; then drained and well dried. When it is perfectly dry, it is then roasted in a plate made for that purpose, ashes being mixed with it to hinder it from burning; and they keep continually stirring it, that it may take only the red colour which they want. When it has taken that colour, they remove the ashes, rub it well, and then put it in a mortar with the ashes of dried stalks of kidney beans, and a little water; they then beat it gently, which quickly breaks the husk, and turns the whole into meal. This meal, after being pounded, is dried in the sun, and after this last operation it may be carried any where, and will keep six months, if care be taken from time to time to expose it to the sun. When they want to eat of it, they mix in a vessel two thirds water with one third meal, and in a few minutes the mixture swells greatly in bulk, and is fit to eat. It is a very nourishing food, and is an excellent provision for travellers, and those who go to any distance to trade.

This parched meal, mixed with milk and a little sugar, may be served up at the best tables. When mixed with milk-chocolate it makes a very lasting nourishment. From Maiz they make a strong and agreeable beer; and they likewise distil brandy from it.

Wheat, rye, barley, and oats grow extremely well in Louisiana; but I must add one precaution in regard to wheat; when it is sown by itself, as in France, it grows at first wonderfully; but when it is in flower, a great number of drops of red water may be observed at the bottom of the stalk within six inches of the ground, which are collected there during the night, and disappear at sun-rising. This water is of such an acrid nature, that in a short time it consumes the stalk, and the ear falls before the grain is formed. To prevent this misfortune, which is owing to the too great richness of the soil, the method I have taken, and which has succeeded extremely well, is to mix with the wheat you intend to sow, some rye and dry mould, in such a proportion that the mould shall be equal to the rye and wheat together. This method I remember to have seen practised in France; and when I asked the reason of it, the farmer told me that as the land was new, and had lately been a wood, it contained an acid that was prejudicial to the wheat; and that as the rye absorbed that acid without being hurt, it thereby preserved the other grain. I have seen barley and oats in that country three feet high.

The rice which is cultivated in that country was brought from Carolina. It succeeds surprizingly well, and experience has there proved, contrary to the common notion, that it does not want to have its foot always in the water. It has been sown in the flat country without being flooded, and the grain that was reaped was full grown, and of a very delicate taste. The fine relish need not surprise us; for it is so with all plants and fruits that grow without being watered, and at a distance from watery places. Two crops may be reaped from the same plant; but the second is poor if it be not flooded. I know not whether they have attempted, since I left Louisiana, to sow it upon the sides of hills.

The first settlers found in the country French-beans of various colours, particularly red and black, and they have been called beans of forty days, because they require no longer time to grow and to be fit to eat green. The Apalachean beans are so called because we received them from a nation of the natives of that name. They probably had them from the English of Carolina, whither they had been brought from Guinea. Their stalks spread upon the ground to the length of four or five feet. They are like the other beans, but much smaller, and of a brown colour, having a black ring round the eye, by which they are joined to the shell. These beans boil tender, and have a tolerable relish, but they are sweetish, and somewhat insipid.

The potatoes are roots more commonly long than thick; their form is various, and their fine skin is like that of the Topinambous (Irish potatoes.) In their substance and taste they very much resemble sweet chesnuts. They are cultivated in the following manner; the earth is raised in little hills or high furrows about a foot and a half broad, that by draining the moisture, the roots may have a better relish. The small potatoes being cut in little pieces with an eye in each, four or five of those pieces are planted on the head of the hills. In a short time they push out shoots, and these shoots being cut off about the middle of August within seven or eight inches of the ground, are planted double, cross-ways, in the crown of other hills. The roots of these last are the most esteemed, not only on account of their fine relish, but because they are easier kept during the winter. In order to preserve them during that season, they dry them in the sun as soon as they are dug up, and then lay them up in a close and dry place, covering them first with ashes, over which they lay dry mould. They boil them, or bake them, or roast them on hot coals like chesnuts; but they have the finest relish when baked or roasted. They are eat dry, or cut into small slices in milk without sugar, for they are sweet of themselves. Good sweetmeats are also made of them, and some Frenchmen have drawn brandy from them.

The Cushaws are a kind of pompion. There are two sorts of them, the one round, and the other in the shape of a hunting horn. These last are the best, being of a more firm substance, which makes them keep much better than the others; their sweetness is not so insipid, and they have fewer seeds. They make sweetmeats of these last, and use both kinds in soup; they make fritters of them, fry them, bake them, and roast them on the coals, and in all ways of cooking they are good and palatable.

All kinds of melons grow admirably well in Louisiana. Those of Spain, of France, of England, which last are called white melons, are there infinitely finer than in the countries from whence they have their name; but the best of all are the water-melons. As they are hardly known in France, except in Provence, where a few of the small kind grow, I fancy a description of them will not be disagreeable to the reader.

The stalk of this melon spreads like ours upon the ground, and extends to the length of ten feet. It is so tender, that when it is any way bruised by treading upon it, the fruit dies; and if it is rubbed in the least, it grows warm. The leaves are very much indented, as broad as the hand when they are spread out, and are somewhat of a sea-green colour. The fruit is either round like a pompion, or long. There are some good melons of this last kind, but the first sort are most esteemed, and deservedly so. The weight of the largest rarely exceeds thirty pounds, but that of the smallest is always above ten pounds. Their rind is of a pale green colour, interspersed with large white spots. The substance that adheres to the rind is white, crude, and of a disagreeable tartness, and is therefore never eaten. The space within that is filled with a light and sparkling substance, that may be called for its properties a rose-coloured snow. It melts in the mouth as if it were actually snow, and leaves a relish like that of the water prepared for sick people from gooseberry jelly. This fruit cannot fail therefore of being very refreshing, and is so wholesome, that persons in all kinds of distempers may satisfy their appetite with it, without any apprehension of being the worse for it. The water-melons of Africa are not near so relishing as those of Louisiana.

The seeds of water-melons are placed like those of the French melons. Their shape is oval and flat, being as thick at the ends as towards the middle; their length is about six lines, and their breadth four. Some are black and others red; but the black are the best, and it is those you ought to choose for sowing, if you would wish to have good fruit; which you cannot fail of, if they are not planted in strong ground, where they would degenerate and become red.

All kinds of greens and roots which have been brought from

Europe into that colony succeed better there than in France, provided they be planted in a soil suited to them; for it is certainly absurd to think that onions and other bulbous plants should thrive there in a soft and watery soil, when every where else they require a light and dry earth. . . .

In order to give an account of the several sorts of plants cultivated in Louisiana, I begin with Maiz, as being the most useful grain, seeing it is the principal food of the people of America, and that the French found it cultivated by the Indians.

Maiz, which in France we call Turkey corn, (and we Indian-corn) is a grain of the size of a pea; there is of it as large as our sugar-pea: it grows on a sort of husks, (Quenouille) in ascending rows: some of these husks have to the number of seven hundred grains upon them, and I have counted even to a greater number. This husk may be about two inches thick, by seven or eight inches and upwards in length: it is wrapped up in several covers or thin leaves, which screen it from the avidity of birds. Its foot or stalk is often of the same size: it has leaves about two inches and upwards broad, by two feet and a half long, which are chanelled, or formed like gutters, by which they collect the dew which dissolves at sun-rising, and trickles down to the stalk, sometimes in such plenty, as to wet the earth around them for the breadth of six or seven inches. Its flower is on the top of the stalk, which is sometimes eight feet high. We ordinarily find five or six ears on each stalk, and in order to procure a greater crop, the part of the stalk above the ears ought to be cut away.

For sowing the Maiz in a field already cleared and prepared, holes are made four feet asunder every way, observing to make the rows as straight as may be, in order to weed them the easier: into every hole five or six grains are put, which are previously to be steeped for twenty-four hours at least, to make them rise or shoot the quicker, and to prevent the fox and birds from eating such quantities of them: by day there are people to guard them against birds; by night fires are made at proper distances to frighten away the fox, who would otherwise turn up the ground, and eat the corn of all the rows, one after another, without omitting one, till he has his fill, and is therefore the most pernicious animal to this corn. The corn, as soon as shot out of the earth, is weeded: when it mounts up, and its stalks are an inch big, it is hilled, to secure it against the wind. This grain produces enough for two negroes to make fifty barrels, each weighing an hundred and fifty pounds.

Such as begin a plantation in woods, thick set with cane, have an advantage in the Maiz, that makes amends for the labour of clearing the ground; a labour always more fatiguing than cultivating a spot already cleared. The advantage is this: they begin with cutting down the canes for a great extent of ground; the trees they peel two feet high quite round: this operation is performed in the beginning of March, as then the sap is in motion in that country: about fifteen days after, the canes, being dry, are set on fire: the sap of the trees are thereby made to descend, and the branches are burnt, which kills the trees.

On the following day they sow the corn in the manner I have just shewn: the roots of the cane, which are not quite dead, shoot fresh canes, which are very tender and brittle; and as no other weeds grow in the field that year, it is easy to be weeded of these canes, and as much corn again may be made, as in a field already cultivated.

This grain they eat in many different ways; the most common way is to make it into Sagamity, which is a kind of gruel made with water, or strong broth. They bake bread of it like cakes (by baking it over the fire on an iron plate, or on a board before the fire,) which is much better than what they bake in the oven, at least for present use; but you must make it every day; and even then it is too heavy to soak in soup of any kind. They likewise make Parched Meal of it, which is a dish of the natives, as well as the Cooedlou, or bread mixt with beans. The ears of corn roasted are likewise a peculiar dish of theirs; and the small corn dressed in that manner is as agreeable to us as to them. A light and black earth agrees much better with the Maiz than a strong and rich one.

The Parched Meal is the best preparation of this corn; the French like it extremely well, no less than the Indians themselves: I can affirm that it is a very good food, and at the same time the best sort of provision that can be carried on a journey, because it is refreshing and extremely nourishing.

As for the small Indian corn, you may see an account of it in the first chapter of the third Book; where you will likewise find an account of the way of sowing wheat, which if you do not observe, you may as well sow none.

Rice is sown in a soil well laboured, either by the plough or hoe, and in winter, that it may be sowed before the time of the inundation. It is sown in furrows of the breadth of a hoe: when shot, and three or four inches high, they let water into the furrows, but in a small quantity, in proportion as it grows, and then give water in greater plenty.

The ear of this grain nearly resembles that of oats; its grains are fastened to a beard, and its chaff is very rough, and full of those fine and hard beards: the bran adheres not to the grain, as that of the corn of France; it consists of two lobes, which easily separate and loosen, and are therefore readily cleaned and broke off.

They eat their rice as they do in France, but boiled much thicker, and with much less cookery, although it is not inferior in goodness to ours: they only wash it in warm water, taken out of the same pot you are to boil it in, then throw it in all at once, and boil it till it bursts, and so it is dressed without any further trouble. They make bread of it that is very white and of a good relish; but they have tried in vain to make any that will soak in soup.

The culture of the Water-melon is simple enough. They choose for the purpose a light soil, as that of a rising ground, well exposed: they make holes in the earth, from two and a half to three feet in diameter, and distant from each other fifteen feet every way, in each of which holes they put five or six seeds. When the seeds are come up, and the young plants have struck out five or six leaves, the four most thriving plants are pitched upon, and the others plucked up to prevent their starving each other, when too numerous. It is only at that time that they have the trouble of watering them, nature alone performing the rest, and bringing them to maturity; which is known by the green rind beginning to change colour. There is no occasion to cut or prune them. The other species of melons are cultivated in the same manner, only that between the holes the distance is but five or six feet.

All sorts of garden plants and greens thrive extremely well in Louisiana, and grow in much greater abundance than in France: the climate is warmer, and the soil much better. However, it is to be observed, that onions and other bulbous plants answer not in the low lands, without a great deal of pains and labour; whereas in the high grounds they grow very large and of a fine flavour.

DOCUMENT 6:

Engravings by Jacques Le Moyne de Morques Depict Native American Subsistence Strategies in Sixteenth-Century Florida

Sources: Library of Congress, Print and
Photographs Division, reproductions
#LC-US262–31871 and #LC-US262–31869.

French artist Jacque Le Moyne de Morques traveled to Florida in 1564 with explorer René de Laudonnière, who established Fort Caroline near Jacksonville in 1565. Le Moyne documented the French efforts to build a colony using his artistic skill, but he lost much of his work in an attack by their Spanish rivals in 1565. Upon returning to Europe he reproduced many of his sketches from memory. Engraver Theodor de Bry popularized his efforts when he published a number of engravings based upon Le Moyne's drawings in 1591. Among other topics, these engravings document the culture of the local Timucua Indians. However, due to the nature of their creation, the drawings cannot be interpreted as entirely reliable depictions of the local population. These images purport to document the hunting and agricultural techniques of the Timucua.

Bon jhrer Hirschjacht. XXV.

 IE Indianer brauchen eine solche Geschicklichkeyt / Hirsche zu fangen / dergleichen wir zuvor nie gesehen. Die Häute der allergrössesten Hirsche / so sie jemals gefangen / legen sie so geschicklich an Leib / daß sie das Theyl / so dem Hirsch am Kopff gestanden / auch über ihren Kopff ziehen / damit sie durch die Augenlöcher / gleich als durch eine Laruen / sehen können / Wann sie sich nun also angethan / gehen sie so nahe / als jnen müglich / zun Hirschen (so sich im geringsten dafür nicht scheuwen) hinzu / doch daß sie der Zeit warnemmen / zu welcher die Hirsche an das Wasser zu trincken kommen / welche sie nachmals leichtlich mit Bogen / sampt den Pfeilen / so sie in den Händen haben / schiessen können / dieweil jrer in diesem Lande sehr viel sind. Damit sie aber im schiessen / am lincken Arme / durch die Sehnen deß Bogens / nit verletzt werden / verwaren sie denselben mit einer Rinden von einm Baum / wie sie das die Natur unterwiesen. Die Hirschhäute aber / welche sie jhnen abziehen / können sie ohne Stahel / nur mit Muscheln / so artig bereyten / daß es zu verwundern / Und ich halte dar-
für / daß niemande in gantz Europa zu finden sey / der diese Häute
kunstreicherer wisse zu bereyten / als
eben sie.

G iij   Wie sie

Document 6

Document 6

CHAPTER 2

Colonial Culinary Encounters

Culinary historian Jessica B. Harris has observed that in tracing the origins of American cuisine "three is a magic number." Native American and European cultural encounters ultimately altered the eating habits of both groups. African arrivals to North America added a transformative third layer of culinary knowledge. They exchanged not only recipes and cooking techniques but also biological specimens. In what has become known as the Columbian Exchange, plants from the Americas, most notably maize, were taken to Europe and Africa, and European and African plants such as wheat and okra were planted in the Americas.

The documents in this chapter reveal how African, European, and Native American food habits were disrupted and transformed during the era of colonization. A combination of European and African foods nourished the involuntary passengers of the slave ships that made the brutal journey across the Atlantic. The rations fed to enslaved Africans on their transatlantic journey are described in document 3, a testimonial by Alexander Falconbridge, a surgeon who worked on slave-trading vessels. The foodways of the New World were created in the context of suffering and displacement that also impacted Native Americans. European settlers initially relied upon the Indians for food, but in spite of this dependence, they put mechanisms into place to disrupt traditional forms of subsistence. In the colonial period, Europeans were hardly immune to their own culinary distress as they endeavored to find ample and satisfying food in an unfamiliar environment. Documents 6 and 9 describe the hunger of English colonists in Virginia in the early seventeenth century.

Englishman John Gerarde Evaluates the Nutritional Value of Maize, 1597

Source: John Gerarde, *The Herball or Generall Historie of Plantes* (London: John Norton, 1597), 76–77.

Englishman John Gerarde's massive 1597 The Herball or Generall Historie of Plantes *contains almost 1,500 pages of text and reflects the state of contemporary European botanical knowledge. His analysis includes a number of plants that had been introduced to Europe as part of the Columbian Exchange, including potatoes, tomatoes, and maize. Gerarde's descriptions reveal a degree of culinary xenophobia and suspicion of the unfamiliar. Tomatoes, he observes, have a "ranke and stinking savour." In this section he argues that American maize is an uncivilized grain better suited for animal consumption than for the human table.*

Turky wheate doth nourish far lesse than either Wheate, Rie, Barly or Otes. The bread which is made thereof is meanly white, withougt bran: it is hard and drie as biskit is, and hath in it no clamminess at all: for which cause it is hard digestion, and yeeldeth to the body little or no nourishment, it slowly descendeth and bindeth the belly, as that doth which is made of Mill or Panick. We have as yet no certain proofe or experience concerning the vertues of this kinde of Corne, although the barbarous Indians which know no better, are constrained to make a virtue of necessitie, and think it a good food; whereas we may easily judge that it nourisheth but little, and is of hard and evil digestion, a more convenient food for swine than for men.

1 *Frumentum Asiaticum.*Corne of Asia.   2 *Frumentum Turcicum.* Turkie Corne.

The forme of the eares of Turkie Wheate.

3 *Frumenti Indici spica.*   4 *Frumentum Indicum album.*
Turkie Wheate in the huske, as also naked or bare.   The eare of white Turkie Wheate.

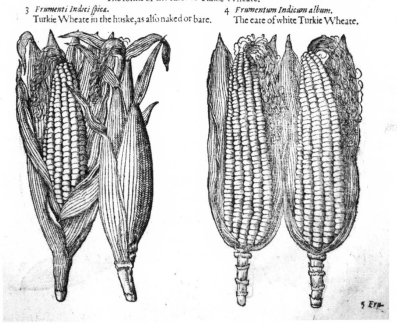

Document 1

Olaudah Equiano Describes the Food of Seventeenth-Century Igbo

---

Source: Olaudah Equiano, *The Interesting Life of Olaude Equiano or Gustavus Vassa, the African* (1789).

In his autobiography, published in London in 1789, Olaudah Equiano describes being captured from his village in West Africa and being subjected to the horrors of the transatlantic slave trade. In this passage Equiano describes the food habits of his native home. His evocative and remarkable chronicle has undergone intensive scrutiny since 2005, when literary scholar Vincent Carretta discovered evidence that suggests that Equiano may have been born in South Carolina and not in present-day Nigeria as he claimed.

That part of Africa, known by the name of Guinea, to which the trade for slaves is carried on, extends along the coast above 3400 miles, from the Senegal to Angola, and includes a variety of kingdoms. Of these the most considerable is the kingdom of Benen, both as to extent and wealth, the richness and cultivation of the soil, the power of its king, and the number and warlike disposition of the inhabitants. It is situated nearly under the line, and extends along the coast about 170 miles, but runs back into the interior part of Africa to a distance hitherto I believe unexplored by any traveller; and seems only terminated at length by the empire of Abyssinia, near 1500 miles from its beginning. This kingdom is divided into many provinces or districts: in one of the most remote and fertile of which, called Eboe, I was born, in the year 1745, in a charming fruitful vale, named Essaka. The distance of this province from the capital of Benin and the sea coast must be very considerable; for I had never heard of white men or Europeans, nor of the sea. . . .

    Our manner of living is entirely plain; for as yet the natives are unacquainted with those refinements in cookery which debauch the taste: bullocks, goats, and poultry, supply the greatest part of their food. These constitute likewise the principal wealth of the country, and the chief articles of its commerce. The flesh is usually stewed in a pan; to make it savoury we sometimes use also pepper, and other spices, and we have salt made of wood ashes. Our vegetables are mostly plantains, eadas, yams, beans, and Indian corn. The head of the family usually eats alone; his wives and slaves have also their separate tables. Before we taste food we always wash our hands: indeed our cleanliness on all occasions is extreme; but on this it is an indispensable ceremony. After washing, libation is made, by pouring out a small portion of the food, in a certain place, for the spirits of departed relations, which the natives suppose to preside over their conduct, and guard them from evil. They are totally unacquainted with strong or spirituous liquours; and their principal beverage is palm wine. This is gotten from a tree of that name by tapping it at the top, and fastening a large gourd to it; and sometimes one tree will yield three or four gallons in a night. When just drawn it is of a most delicious sweetness; but in a few days it acquires a tartish and more spirituous flavour: though I never saw any one intoxicated by it. The same tree also produces nuts and oil. . . .

Our land is uncommonly rich and fruitful, and produces all kinds of vegetables in great abundance. We have plenty of Indian corn, and vast quantities of cotton and tobacco. Our pine apples grow without culture; they are about the size of the largest sugar-loaf, and finely flavoured. We have also spices of different kinds, particularly pepper; and a variety of delicious fruits which I have never seen in Europe; together with gums of various kinds, and honey in abundance. All our industry is exerted to improve those blessings of nature. Agriculture is our chief employment; and every one, even the children and women, are engaged in it. Thus we are all habituated to labour from our earliest years. Every one contributes something to the common stock; and as we are unacquainted with idleness, we have no beggars. The benefits of such a mode of living are obvious. . . .

Our tillage is exercised in a large plain or common, some hours walk from our dwellings, and all the neighbours resort thither in a body. They use no beasts of husbandry; and their only instruments are hoes, axes, shovels, and beaks, or pointed iron to dig with. Sometimes we are visited by locusts, which come in large clouds, so as to darken the air, and destroy our harvest. This however happens rarely, but when it does, a famine is produced by it. I remember an instance or two wherein this happened. This common is often the theatre of war; and therefore when our people go out to till their land, they not only go in a body, but generally take their arms with them for fear of a surprise; and when they apprehend an invasion they guard the avenues to their dwellings, by driving sticks into the ground, which are so sharp at one end as to pierce the foot, and are generally dipt in poison. From what I can recollect of these battles, they appear to have been irruptions of one little state or district on the other, to obtain prisoners or booty. . . . Those prisoners which were not sold or redeemed we kept as slaves: but how different was their condition from that of the slaves in the West Indies! With us they do no more work than other members of the community, even their masters; their food, clothing and lodging were nearly the same as theirs, (except that they were not permitted to eat with those who were free-born); and there was scarce any other difference between them, than a superior degree of importance which the head of a family possesses in our state, and that authority which, as such, he exercises over every part of his household. Some of these slaves have even slaves under them as their own property, and for their own use. . . .

Such is the imperfect sketch my memory has furnished me with of the manners and customs of a people among whom I first drew my breath.

DOCUMENT 3:

Alexander Falconbridge Describes the Food of the Middle Passage

Source: Alexander Falconbridge, *An Account of the Slave Trade on the Coast of Africa* (London: J. Phillips, 1788), 21–23.

Alexander Falconbridge worked as a surgeon in the slave trade, using his medical knowledge to keep the valuable human cargo alive and salable. His experiences onboard slavers eroded his initial acquiescence to the system of human bondage. He became a supporter of the abolitionist movement and wrote vividly about the psychological and physical suffering of enslaved people. In this excerpt he describes the food served on the transatlantic voyage and reveals that the system of chattel slavery sought to control all human volition, including the most basic decision about whether or not to eat.

The diet of the negroes, while on board, consists chiefly of horse-beans, boiled to the consistence of a pulp, of boiled yams and rice, and sometimes of a small quantity of beef or pork. The latter are frequently taken from the provisions laid in for the sailors. They sometimes make use of a sauce, composed of palm-oil, mixed with flour, water, and pepper, which the sailors call slabber-sauce. Yams are the favourite food of the Eboe, or Bight negroes, and rice or corn, of those from the Gold and Windward Coasts; each preferring the produce of their native soil.

In their own country, the negroes in general live on animal food and fish, with roots, yams, and Indian corn. The horse-beans and rice, with which they are fed aboard ship, are chiefly taken from Europe. The latter, indeed, is sometimes purchased on the coast, being far superior to any other.

The Gold Coast negroes scarcely ever refuse any food that is offered them, and they generally eat larger quantities of whatever is placed before them, than any other species of negroes, whom they likewise excel in strength of body and mind. Most of the slaves have such an aversion to the horse-beans that unless they are narrowly watched, when fed upon deck, they will throw them overboard, or in each other's faces when they quarrel.

They are commonly fed twice a day, about eight o'clock in the morning and four in the afternoon. In most ships they are only fed with their own food once a day. Their food is served up to them in tubs, about the size of a small water bucket. They are placed round these tubs in companies of ten to each tub, out of which they feed themselves with wooden spoons. These they soon lose, and when they are not allowed others, they feed themselves with their hands. In favourable weather they are fed upon deck, but in bad weather their food is given them below. Numberless quarrels take place among them during their meals, more especially when they are put upon short allowance, which frequently happens, if the passage from the coast of Guinea to the West-India islands, proves of unusual length. In that case, the weak are obliged to be content with a very scanty portion. Their allowance of water is about half a pint each at every meal. It is handed round in a bucket, and given to each negroe in a pannekin; a small utensil with a strait handle somewhat similar to a sauce-boat, However, when the ships approach the islands with a favourable breeze, they are no longer restricted.

Upon the negroes refusing to take sustenance, I have seen coals of fire, glowing hot, put on a shovel, and placed so near their lips, as to scorch and burn them. And this has been accompanied with threats, of forcing them to swallow the coals, if they any longer persisted in refusing to eat. These means have generally had the desired effect. I have also been credibly informed, that a certain captain in the slave trade, poured melted lead on such of the negroes as obstinately refused their food.

DOCUMENT 4:

Colonial Advertisement Offering Slaves for Sale Who Had Experience Cultivating Rice

Source: Library of Congress, Prints and Photographs Division, reproduction #LC-US262–10293.

By the turn of the eighteenth century, European settlers in Carolina had begun growing what was to become the primary staple crop of the local plantation economy: rice. This grain was cultivated using many West African agricultural techniques. For example, the baskets used in winnowing, the process of separating the hull from the grain, were nearly identical to those used in Africa. White planters were so cognizant of their dependency on African knowledge and skill that they were willing to pay higher prices for slaves who came from rice-growing regions of the continent.

TO BE SOLD on board the ship *Bance-Island*, on Tuesday the 6th of *May* next, at *Ashley-Ferry*; a choice cargo of about 250 fine healthy NEGROES, just arrived from the Windward & Rice Coast—The utmost care has already been taken, and shall be continued, to keep them free from the least danger of being infected with the SMALL-POX, no boat having been on board, and all other communication with the people from *Charles-Town* prevented.

Austin, Laurens, & Appleby

DOCUMENT 5:

Wahunsonacock Advises the English Residents of Jamestown Not to Steal Food from Native Americans

Source: Edward Arber, ed., *Travels and Works of Captain John Smith* (Edinburgh: John Grant, 1910), 132–36.

The English founded their first permanent settlement in North America at Jamestown, Virginia, in 1607. The Chesapeake region was home to about fourteen thousand Algonquian-speaking Powhatan Indians who were led by a chief named Wahunsonacock, whom the English referred to as "Chief Powhatan." The Europeans were more intent on finding ways to exploit the environment to gain quick wealth than they were in becoming self-sustaining. For food, they originally relied on provisions brought from Europe and the generosity of the Native Americans, who gave them items such as oysters, beans, and wild fruit and traded with them for maize. Eventually, the Powhatan could no longer satisfy the seemingly insatiable hunger of the English, and the colonists burned Indian villages and seized provisions. Wahunsonacock urged the English

not to persist in this shortsighted and violent approach to
feeding themselves.

Captain Smith, you may understand that I, having seen the death of all my people thrice, and not one living of those 3 generations but my self, I know the difference of peace and war better then any in my Country. But now I am old, and ere long must die. My brethren, namely Opichapam, Opechankanough, and Kekataugh, my two sisters, and their two daughters, are distinctly each others successors. I wish their experience no less then mine, and your love to them, no less then mine to you: but this brute from Nansamund, that you are come to destroy my Country, so much affrighted all my people, as they dare not visit you. What will it avail you to take that perforce, you may quietly have with love, or to destroy them that provide you food? What can you get by war, when we can hide our provision and flie to the woods, whereby you must famish, by wronging us your friends? And why are you thus jealous of our loves, seeing us unarmed, and both doe, and are willing still to feed you with that you cannot get but by our labors? Think you I am so simple not to know it is better to eat good meat, lie well, and sleep quietly with my women and children, laugh, and be merry with you, have copper, hatchets, or what I want being your friend; then bee forced to fly from all, to lie cold in the woods, feed upon acorns roots and such trash, and be so hunted by you that I can neither rest eat nor sleep, but my tired men must watch, and if a twig but break, every one cry, there comes Captain Smith: then must I fly I know not whether and thus with miserable fear end my miserable life, leaving my pleasures to such youths as you, which, through your rash unadvisedness, may quickly as miserably end, for want of that you never know how to find? Let this therefore assure you of our loves, and every year our friendly trade shall furnish you with corn; and now also if you would come in friendly manner to us, and not thus with your guns and swords, as to invade your foes.

Captain John Smith Describes the Starving Time of 1609–1610

Source: John Smith, *The Generall Historie of Virginia, New England & The Summer Isles* (London: Michael Sparks, 1624), 105–6.

Captain John Smith instituted military-style discipline in Jamestown, the first permanent English colony in North America, which was plagued by food scarcity in its early years. He forced the colonists to engage in hunting and in agriculture and traded with the Powhatan Indians for food. In the fall of 1609, Smith returned to England for medical care for a wound caused by a gunpowder explosion. After his departure the colonists endured a period of extreme hunger exacerbated by drought and hostilities with their Powhatan trading partners. Conditions were so extreme that they resorted to eating snakes, rats, dogs, and cats, and even to cannibalism. By the end of the winter only sixty out of five hundred colonists had survived.

The day before Captaine Smith returned for England with the ships, Captaine Davis arrived in a small Pinace, with some sixteene proper men more: To these were added a company from James towne, under the command of Captaine John Sickelmore alias Ratliffe, to inhabit Point Comfort. Captaine Martin and Captaine West, having lost their boats and neere halfe their men among the Salvages, were returned to James towne; for the Salvages no sooner understood Smith was gone, but they all revolted, and did spoile and murther all they incountered. Now wee were all constrained to live onely on that Smith had onely for his owne Companie, for the rest had consumed their proportions, and now they had twentie Presidents with all their appurtenances: Master Piercie our new President, was so sicke hee could neither goe nor stand. But ere all was consumed, Captaine West and Captaine Sickelmore, each with a small ship and thirtie or fortie men well appointed, sought abroad to trade. Sickelmore upon the confidence of Powhatan, with about thirtie others as carelesse as himselfe, were all slaine, onely Jeffrey Shortridge escaped, and Pokahontas the Kings daughter saved a boy called Henry Spilman, that lived many yeeres after, by her meanes, amongst the Patawomekes. Powhatan still as he found meanes, cut off their Boats, denied them trade, so that Captaine West set saile for England. Now we all found the losse of Captaine Smith, yea his greatest maligners could now curse his losse: as for corne, provision and contribution from the Salvages, we had nothing but mortall wounds, with clubs and arrowes; as for our Hogs, Hens, Goats, Sheepe, Horse, or what lived, our commanders, officers & Salvages daily consumed them, some small proportions sometimes we tasted, till all was devoured; then swords, armes, pieces, or any thing, wee traded with the Salvages, whose cruell fingers were so oft imbrewed in our blouds, that what by their crueltie, our Governours indiscretion, and the losse of our ships, of five hundred within six moneths after Captaine Smiths departure, there remained not past sixtie men, women and children, most miserable and poore creatures; and those were preserved for the most part, by roots, herbes, acornes, walnuts, berries, now and then a little fish: they that had startch in these extremities, made no small use of it; yea, even the very skinnes of our horses. Nay, so great was our famine, that a Salvage we slew, and buried, the poorer sort tooke him up againe and eat him, and so did divers one another boyled and stewed with roots and herbs: And one amongst the rest did kill his wife, powdered her, and had eaten part of her before it was knowne, for which hee was executed, as hee well deserved; now whether shee was better roasted, boyled or carbonado'd, I know not, but of such a dish as powdered wife I never heard of. This was that time, which still to this day we called the starving time; it were too vile to say, and scarce to be beleeved, what we endured: but the occasion was our owne, for want of providence, industrie and government, and not the barrennesse and defect of the Countrie, as is generally supposed; for till then in three yeeres, for the numbers were landed us, we had never from England provision sufficient for six moneths, though it seemed by the bils of loading sufficient was sent us, such a glutton is the Sea, and such good fellowes the Mariners; we as little tasted of the great proportion sent us, as they of our want and miseries, yet notwithstanding they ever over-swayed and ruled the businesse, though we endured all that is said, and chiefly lived on what this good Countrie naturally afforded; yet had wee beene even in Paradice it selfe with these Governours, it would not have beene much better with us; yet there was amongst us, who had they had the government as Captaine Smith appointed, but that they could not maintaine it, would surely have kept us from those extremities of miseries. This in ten daies more, would have supplanted us all with death.

DOCUMENT 7:

The Colonists at Plimoth Plantation Celebrate Their 1621 Harvest

Sources: Edward Winslow and William Bradford, *Mourt's Relation or Journal of the Plantation at Plymouth,* ed. Henry Martin Dexter (Boston: John Kimball Wiggin, 1865), 133; and William Bradford, *Of Plimouth Plantation* (Boston: Wright and Potter Printing, 1898), 127.

The national holiday of Thanksgiving as observed in the United States was a nineteenth-century creation. After a lengthy campaign, Sarah Josepha Hale, editor of the popular magazine Godey's Lady's Book, *convinced President Abraham Lincoln to issue a proclamation in 1863 declaring the last Thursday of November a national holiday. The event has been celebrated continuously each year since. Hale later popularized the idea that the "First Thanksgiving" had occurred in 1621 in Plimoth Plantation when the European settlers and Wampanoag Indians came together for a harvest celebration. Very little is known about the 1621 meal. These two documents provide the only primary source material about who was there and what was consumed. What is certain is that the feast was not an annual event or a direct progenitor of the nineteenth-century celebration.*

Edward Winslow's account:

Our harvest being gotten in, our Governour sent foure men on fowling, that so we might after a speciall manner rejoyce together, after we had gathered the fruits of our labours ; they foure in one day killed as much fowle, as with a little helpe beside, served the Company almost a weeke, at which time amongst other Recreations, we exercised our Armes, many of the Indians coming amongst us, and amongst the rest their greatest king Massasoyt, with some nintie men, whom for three dayes we entertained and feasted, and they went out and killed five Deere, which we brought to the Plantation and bestowed on our Governour, and upon the Captaine and others. And although it be not always so plentifull, as it was at this time with us, yet by the goodnesse of God, we are so farre from want, that we often wish you partakers of our plentie.

William Bradford's account:

They begane now to gather in ye small harvest they had, and to fitte up their houses and dwellings against winter, being all well recovered in health & strenght, and had all things in good plenty; for as some were thus imployed in affairs abroad, others were excersised in fishing, aboute codd, & bass, & other fish, of which yey tooke good store, of which every family had their portion. All ye somer ther was no want. And now begane to come in store of foule, as winter approached, of which this place did abound when they came first (but afterward decreased by degrees). And besids water foule, ther was great store of wild Turkies, of which they tooke many, besids venison, &c. Besids, they had about a peck a meale a weeke to a person, or now since harvest, Indean corn to yt proportion. Which made many afterwards write so largly of their plenty hear to their freinds in England, which were not fained, but true reports.

DOCUMENT 8:

Massachusetts Colonist Mary Rowlandson Describes the Food Eaten by the Algonquin Who Held Her Captive in 1675 and 1676

Source: Mary Rowlandson, *Narrative of the Captivity and Restoration of Mrs. Mary Rowlandson* (1682).

The so-called first Thanksgiving of 1621, a harvest festival jointly attended by English colonists and Wampanoag Indians, is enshrined in the mythology of the United States as an example of interracial cooperation exemplified in the culinary realm. However, the feast was a relative anomaly, and the dominant form of interaction between the settlers and the indigenous people was increasingly hostility. Puritan settler Mary Rowlandson was held captive by Native Americans for eleven weeks during King Philip's War. She was appalled by the eating practices of the Algonquin, whose normal culinary routines had been interrupted by the chaos of war. In this passage she marvels at the ingenuity of her captors and at the fact that God enabled them to find sufficient nourishment to survive.

It was thought, if their corn were cut down, they would starve and die with hunger, and all their corn that could be found, was destroyed, and they driven from that little they had in store, into the woods in the midst of winter; and yet how to admiration did the Lord preserve them for His holy ends, and the destruction of many still amongst the English! strangely did the Lord provide for them; that I did not see (all the time I was among them) one man, woman, or child, die with hunger.

Though many times they would eat that, that a hog or a dog would hardly touch; yet by that God strengthened them to be a scourge to His people.

The chief and commonest food was ground nuts. They eat also nuts and acorns, artichokes, lilly roots, ground beans, and several other weeds and roots, that I know not.

They would pick up old bones, and cut them to pieces at the joints, and if they were full of worms and maggots, they would scald them over the fire to make the vermin come out, and then boil them, and drink up the liquor, and then beat the great ends of them in a mortar, and so eat them. They would eat horse's guts, and ears, and all sorts of wild birds which they could catch; also bear, venison, beaver, tortoise, frogs, squirrels, dogs, skunks, rattlesnakes; yea, the very bark of trees; besides all sorts of creatures, and provision which they plundered from the English. I can but stand in admiration to see the wonderful power of God in providing for such a vast number of our enemies in the wilderness, where there was nothing to be seen, but from hand to mouth. Many times in a morning, the generality of them would eat up all they had, and yet have some further supply against they wanted. It is said, "Oh, that my People had hearkened to me, and Israel had walked in my ways, I should have subdued their Enemies and turned my hand against their Adversaries" (Psalm 81.13–14). But now our perverse and evil carriages in the sight of the Lord, have so offended Him, that instead of turning His hand against them, the Lord feeds and nourishes them up to be a scourge to the whole land.

DOCUMENT 9:

An Indentured Servant in Virginia Begs His Parents for Food, 1623

Source: Richard Frethorne, letter to parents, March 20, April 2–3, 1623, in *The Records of the Virginia Company of London*, ed. Susan Kingsbury (Washington, DC: Government Printing Office, 1935), 58–62.

The white colonists in Virginia ultimately depended upon enslaved Africans to meet their enormous demand for cheap labor. However, initially much of the hard work of establishing a settlement was performed by European laborers who agreed to sell their labor for a fixed term in exchange for passage to the Americas and the prospect of starting a new life. In this letter to his parents, Virginia indentured servant Richard Frethorne complains of harsh working conditions and hunger.

LOVING AND KIND FATHER AND MOTHER:

My most humble duty remembered to you, hoping in god of your good health, as I myself am at the making hereof. This is to let you understand that I your child am in a most heavy case by reason of the country, [which] is such that it causeth much sickness, [such] as the scurvy and the bloody flux and diverse other diseases, which maketh the body very poor and weak. And when we are sick there is nothing to comfort us; for since I came out of the ship I never ate anything but peas, and loblollie (that is, water gruel). As for deer or venison I never saw any since I came into this land. There is indeed some fowl, but we are not allowed to go and get it, but must work hard both early and late for a mess of water gruel and a mouthful of bread and beef. A mouthful of bread for a penny loaf must serve for four men which is most pitiful. . . . And I have nothing to comfort me, nor is there nothing to be gotten here but sickness and death. . . . I have not a penny, nor a penny worth, to help me too either spice or sugar or strong waters, without the which one cannot live here. For as strong beer in England doth fatten and strengthen them, so water here doth wash and weaken these here. . . . But I am not half a quarter so strong as I was in England, and all is for want of victuals; for I do protest unto you that I have eaten more in [one] day at home than I have allowed me here for a week. You have given more than my day's allowance to a beggar at the door. . . .

And indeed so I find it now, to my great grief and misery; and [I] saith that if you love me you will redeem me suddenly, for which I do entreat and beg. And if you cannot get the merchants to redeem me for some little money, then for God's sake get a gathering or entreat some good folks to lay out some little sum of money in meal and cheese and butter and beef. Any eating meat will yield great profit. Oil and vinegar is very good; but, father, there is great loss in leaking. But for God's sake send beef and cheese and butter, or the more of one sort and none of another. But if you send cheese, it must be very old cheese; and at the cheesemonger's you may buy very food cheese for twopence farthing or halfpenny, that will be liked very well. But if you send cheese, you must have a care how you pack it in barrels; and you must put cooper's chips between every cheese, or else the heat of the hold will rot them. And look whatsoever you send me—be in never so much—look, what[ever] I make of it, I will deal truly with you. I will send it over and beg the profit to redeem me; and if I die before it come, I have entreated Goodman Jackson to send you the worth of it, who hath promised he will. . . . Good father, do not forget me, but have mercy and pity my miserable case. I know if you did but see me, you would weep to see me; for I have but one suit. . . . Wherefore, for God's sake, pity me . . . good father, send as soon as you can. . . .

Richard Frethorne

CHAPTER 3

Developing
a National Cuisine

Read together, the documents in this chapter yield insights into the nature of early American cuisine. During the colonial era, American food habits were characterized by cultural hybridity due to the combination of cooking techniques and ingredients favored by Native Americans, Europeans, and Africans. However, the foodways of what was to become the United States were not defined by the actual components of the diet alone. "American" food became as much an imagined construct as a tangible cultural creation. From the time of European colonization, many European Americans sought to differentiate their food culture from that of their home countries, which were variously regarded as being sinful, decadent, or undemocratic culinary spaces. Documents 1 and 5 in this chapter demonstrate how American ideas about food consumption were heavily influenced by Puritan ideas. By the time the colonies secured their independence from Great Britain, the concept of a virtuous republican cuisine had emerged. Proponents of American independence—such as Thomas Jefferson, who displays his fondness for American foods in document 8—had announced, according to historian James McWilliams, a "culinary Declaration of Independence."

Cotton Mather Describes Religious Fasting, 1683

Source: Cotton Mather, *Diary of Cotton Mather,*
1681–1708 (Boston: Massachusetts Historical
Society, 1911), 79–80.

Devout Massachusetts Puritans like Cotton Mather
believed that food deprivation and prayer were the means
to obtain spiritual purification and to secure God's bless-
ings. In this passage from his diary, Mather reports fasting
and asking God to help him resist temptation. Frequently,
entire communities observed fast days. Less often, they
enjoyed communal feast days. Puritans were scornful of
the Anglican and Catholic fasting practice where fish was
consumed in the place of other kinds of animal flesh. For
this group, fasting meant abstaining from all forms of
nourishment rather than mere food substitution.

12 d. 11 m. The sorrowful and horrible Vexation, given mee, by such
Temptations of the Divel, as these that I have already mentioned, again
drove mee this Day, to Prayer with Fasting, in secret Places before the
Lord.

I cried unto God, that for the Sake of the Lord Jesus Christ, the
Pollutions of my Soul, might bee *pardoned*, and that I might have the
Spirit of the Lord Jesus Christ, possessing of my Heart, and enabling
mee to serve Him in Holiness, all the Dayes of my Life. I pleaded with
the Lord, that Hee did not use to deny those, who came unto Him,
with such Requests for Grace!

19d. 11 m. Having newly been acquainted, with a tremendous and
an amazing Instance, of a Minister stricken in years, and eminent and
remarked all the Countrey over, for a strict Profession of Holiness, who
yett has lately fallen into those lascivious Violations of the Seventh
Commandment, which have given a most infamous Wound unto
Religion; my Soul was thereby cast into exceeding Fears, lest I, who

am a *young* Man, in my single Estate, should bee left by God, unto some Fall, whereby His Blessed Name would suffer. And this the rather, because I have many Wayes grieved the good Spirit of God; and I am strongly haunted by the evil *Spirit*, with Temptations, that horribly vex my very Soul within mee. For this Cause, I spent this Day, in the mortifying Exercises of a secret *Fast*, with *Prayer*, before the Lord.

As also, that I might obtain a Deliverance for this poor Countrey; which is in extreme Danger of becoming a Prey to *unreasonable* Men, *that have no* Faith.

I Likewise carried the wounded Minister, in my Prayers unto the Lord for all seasonable Mercies to bee vouchsafed him.

23 d. 11 m. The young people of our Congregation, kept this as a Day of Thanksgiving, together; for the Success of the Gospel here; and for the Lives of my Father, and my wretched Self, who dispense it.

The Lord helped mee to preach unto them almost three Hours (tho' I had Uttle more than one Hour's Time to praepare for it) on Act. 11, 21. And a good Day it was!

9 d. 12 m. My extraordinary Occasion for Fasting and Praying still continuing, I did again sett apart this Day, to bee therein spent, secretly before the Lord!

And indeed, little memorable attended mee, all the latter part of the year; except this,—that the Distempers of my Heart, enraged by the Temptations of a filthy Divel, drove mee to the macerating Exercises, of much, *Prayer* with *Fasting* before God. For, I exceedingly trembled, lest I should so grieve the *Holy Spirit*, as to bee left unto something or other, whereby His glorious Name would bee dishonoured; which was the Thing that I deprecated, above all the Plagues in the world. And I resolved, that I would never leave crying unto the Lord, until I had obtained from Him, the Grace to serve Him, with such Holiness, that so much as an ugly Thought, should not once dare to expect any Lodging in my Soul.

DOCUMENT 2:

Changing Fireplace Technology

Sources: Library of Congress, Prints and
Photographs Division, reproductions #HABS
PA, 23-DILV-1–8 and #LC-USZC4–6322.

*In the seventeenth and eighteenth centuries, American
fireplaces were so deep and wide that a cook could often
stand inside of them. These large fireplaces were spacious
enough to contain fires of different temperatures that could
be used to cook multiple dishes simultaneously. They were,
however, inefficient. They rapidly consumed wood, and
a great deal of heat escaped through the large openings.
In 1796, Benjamin Thompson, or Count Rumford, as he
became known, invented a fireplace with a smaller opening and chimney that used less fuel and radiated more
heat than earlier versions.*

Document 2

Document 2

Sarah Kemble Knight Describes Dining during a 1704 Journey from Boston to New Haven

Source: Sarah Kemble Knight, "The Journal of Madam Knight," in *The Puritans*, ed. Perry Miller and Thomas H. Johnson (New York: American Book Company, 1938).

In the eighteenth century, Americans ate most of their meals at home, dining out only while traveling. The food that was served to a captive audience without other options was often indifferently prepared. Sarah Kemble Knight, a teacher from Boston, traveled to New York in 1704 and kept a diary where she recorded her unfavorable impressions of the food served at the taverns and inns she visited on her journey.

MONDAY, Octb'r. ye second, 1704.—About three o'clock afternoon, I begun my Journey from Boston to New-Haven; being about two Hundred Mile. My Kinsman, Capt. Robert Luist, waited on me as farr as Dedham, where I was to meet ye Western post. . . .

Tuesday, October ye third, about 8 in the morning, I with the Post proceeded forward without observing any thing remarkable; And about two, on, Arrived at the Post's second stage, where the western Post mett him and exchanged Letters. Here, having called for something to eat, ye woman bro't in a Twisted thing like a cable, but something whiter; and laying it on the bord, tugg'd for life to bring it into a capacity to spread; wch having wth great pains accomplished, shee serv'd in a dish of Pork and Cabage, I suppose the remains of Dinner. The sause was of a deep Purple, wch I tho't was boil'd in her dye Kettle; the bread was Indian, and every thing on the Table service Agreeable to these. I, being hungry, gott a little down; but my stomach was soon cloy'd, and what cabbage I swallowed serv'd me for a Cudd the whole day after. . . .

. . . From hence wee went pretty briskly forward, and arriv'd at Saybrook ferry about two of the Clock afternoon; and crossing it, wee call'd at an Inn to Bait, (foreseeing we should not have such another Opportunity till we come to Killingsworth.) Landlady come in, with her hair about her ears, and hands at full pay scratching. Shee told us shee had some mutton wch shee would broil, wch I was glad to hear; But I supose forgot to wash her scratchers; in a little time shee brot it in; but it being pickled, and my Guide said it smelt strong of head sause, we left it, and pd sixpence a piece for our Dinners, wch was only smell. . . .

There are great plenty of Oysters all along by the sea side, as farr as I Rode in the Collony, and those very good. And they Generally lived very well and comfortably in their famelies. But too Indulgent (especially ye farmers) to their slaves: sufering too great familiarity from them, permitting ym to sit at Table and eat with them, (as they say to save time,) and into the dish goes the black hoof as freely as the white hand.

DOCUMENT 4:

Cartoon Depicting Colonial Response to the British Tax on Tea, 1774

Source: Library of Congress, Prints and Photographs Division, reproduction #LC-USZC4–14078.

One of the issues that led many American colonists to desire independence from Great Britain was that of taxation. The Townshend Revenue Acts of 1767 placed import duties on a number of items consumed in the colonies, including tea. Patriotic and price-conscious consumers responded by purchasing smuggled tea. The Tea Act of 1773 was designed to rescue the financially ailing East India Company by allowing it to sell tea directly to the colonies without first paying a British duty. Even after the Townshend tax was paid, this legal tea was cheaper than or comparable to the price of smuggled tea. Nonetheless, many refused to comply with the law on the grounds that

Document 4

*Great Britain had no right to impose taxes on the colonies.
In this drawing, angry colonists pour a pot of tea down the
throat of an excise officer who has also been tarred and
feathered. In the background, participants in the Boston
Tea Party are shown dumping forty-five tons of East India
Company tea into the harbor.*

DOCUMENT 5:

New York Coffeehouse, 1797

Source: Library of Congress, Prints and
Photographs Division, reproduction
#LC-USZ62–98020.

*Although tea was the most popular hot beverage of colo-
nial America, coffee became increasingly popular beginning in the late eighteenth century. After the Boston Tea
Party it was seen as a more patriotic beverage. John
Adams resolutely declared that tea had to be "universally
renounced." By the era of the American Revolution, cities
including Boston, New York, and Philadelphia contained
coffeehouses modeled on those in London, where men
gathered to socialize and conduct business. As revolutionary fervor spread, coffeehouses became popular meeting
places for discussing strategies to achieve independence.*

Document 5

Excerpts from the First American Cookbook

Source: Amelia Simmons, *American Cookery*
(Hartford: Hudson and Goodwin, 1796).

American Cookery, by Amelia Simmons, appeared in 1796 and became the first published cookbook written by an American. Much of the book strongly resembles contemporary English cookbooks, and some of the recipes were copied verbatim from other texts. However, the book is distinctive due to its use of ingredients from the Americas, including cranberries, pumpkins, and cornmeal.

Preface

As this treatise is calculated for the improvement of the rising generation of *Females* in America, the Lady of fashion and fortune will not be displeased, if many hints are suggested for the more general and universal knowledge of those females in this country, who by the loss of their parents, or other unfortunate circumstances, are reduced to the necessity of going into families in the line of domestics, or taking refuge with their friends or relations, and doing those things which are really essential to the perfecting them as good wives, and useful members of society. The orphan, tho' left to the care of virtuous guardians, will find it essentially necessary to have an opinion and determination of her own. The world, and the fashion thereof, is so variable, that old people cannot accommodate themselves to the various changes and fashions which daily occur; *they* will adhere to the fashion of *their* day, and will not surrender their attachments to the *good old way*—while the young and the gay, bend and conform readily to the taste of the times, and fancy of the hour. By having an opinion and determination, I would not be understood to mean an obstinate perseverance in trifles, which borders on obstinacy—by no means, but only an adherence to those rules and maxims which have flood the test of ages, and will forever establish the *female character*, a virtuous character—altho' they conform to the ruling taste of the age in cookery, dress, language, manners, &c.

It must ever remain a check upon the poor solitary orphan, that while those females who have parents, or brothers, or riches, to defend their indiscretions, that the orphan must depend solely upon *character*. How immensely important, therefore, that every action, every word, every thought, be regulated by the strictest purity, and that every movement meet the approbation of the good and wise.

The candor of the American Ladies is solicitously intreated by the Authoress, as she is circumscribed in her knowledge, this being an original work in this country. Should any future editions appear, she hopes to render it more valuable. . . .

A Nice Indian Pudding.

No. 1. 3 pints scalded milk, 7 spoons fine Indian meal, stir well together while hot, let stand till cooled; add 7 eggs, half pound raisins, 4 ounces butter, spice and sugar, bake one and half hour.

No. 2. 3 pints scalded milk to one pint meal salted; cool, add 2 eggs, 4 ounces butter, sugar or molasses and spice q. f. it will require two and half hours baking.

No. 3. Salt a pint meal, wet with one quart milk, sweeten and put into a strong cloth, brass or bell metal vessel, stone or earthern pot, secure from wet and boil 12 hours. . . .

Pompkin.

No. 1. One quart stewed and strained, 3 pints cream, 9 beaten eggs, sugar, mace, nutmeg and ginger, laid into paste No. 7 or 3, and with a dough spur, cross and chequer it, and baked in dishes three quarters of an hour.

No. 2. One quart of milk, 1 pint pompkin, 4 eggs, molasses, allspice and ginger in a crust, bake 1 hour.

Benjamin Franklin Gives Advice about Eating and Drinking in *Poor Richard's Almanack*

Source: Benjamin Franklin, *Poor Richard's Almanack* (Waterloo, IA: U.S.C. Publishing Co., 1914).

Between 1732 and 1738, Benjamin Franklin published an annual volume of Poor Richard's Almanack, *which contained items such as weather forecasts, advice, and puzzles. These excerpts from the almanac encapsulate contemporary wisdom about proper dietary habits, which were derived from Puritan ideas about avoiding bodily excess. As a young man, Franklin endeavored to follow his own advice, but in middle age he began eating and drinking more heavily and was afflicted by gout, an illness associated with a rich diet and alcohol consumption.*

A full belly is the mother of all evil.

A full belly makes a dull brain.

Cheese and salt meat should be sparingly eat.

Drunkenness, that worst of evils, makes some men fools, some beasts, some devils.

Drink does not drown care, but waters it, and makes it grow faster.

Drink water; put the money in your pocket, and leave the dry-bellyache in the punch-bowl.

Eat few suppers, and you'll need few medicines.

He that never eats too much, will never be lazy.

He that would travel much, should eat little.

I saw few die of hunger, of eating 100,000.

He that spills the rum loses that only; he that drinks it, often loses both that and himself.

When the wine enters, out goes the truth.

Women and wine, game and deceit, make the wealth small and the wants great.

Youth is pert and positive, age modest and doubting; so ears of corn when young and light, stand bolt upright, but hang their heads when weighty, full, and ripe.

DOCUMENT 8:

Thomas Jefferson Requests American Food while Living in France

Source: "Thomas Jefferson to Nicholas Lewis, September 17, 1787," Thomas Jefferson Papers, Series 1, General Correspondence, 1651–1827, Library of Congress, Manuscript Division.

Thomas Jefferson served as the United States minister to France from 1785 to 1789, an experience that cemented his lifelong passion for French food. His admiration for the nation's cuisine was so well known that Patrick Henry snidely accused him of having "abjured his native victuals." However, this 1787 letter written to his Virginia neighbor Nicholas Lewis demonstrates that Jefferson savored many American traditions too. He craved his native foods even while living in Paris. Jefferson's respect for the food habits of both countries was evident at the table at his Virginia home of Monticello, where the menu was, according to Daniel Webster, "half Virginian, half French."

Paris Sep. 17. 1787
Dear Sir.

. . . I cultivate in my own garden here Indian corn for the use of my own table, to eat green in our manner. But the species I am able to get here for seed, is hard, with a thick skin, and dry. I had at Monticello a species of small white rare ripe corn which we called Homony-corn, and of which we used to make about 20 barrels a year for table use, green, in homony, and in bread. Great George will know well what kind I mean. I wish it were possible for me to receive an ear of this in time for the next year. I think too it might be done if you would be so good as to find an opportunity of sending one to Mr. Madison at New York, and another to Mr. A. Donald at Richmond. More at your leisure I would ask you to send me also an ear of two of the drying corn from the Cherokee country, some best watermelon seeds, some fine Cantaloupe melon seeds, seeds of the common sweet potato (I mean the real seeds and not the root which cannot be brought here without rotting) an hundred or two acorns of the willow oak and about a peck of acorns of the ground oak or dwarf oak, of the kind that George gathered for me one year upon the barrens of buck island creek. As these will be of some bulk, I will ask the favor of you to send them to Mr. Donald at Richmond who will find a conveiance for them to Havre. Perhaps I should do better to trouble Mrs. Lewis with this commission; I therefore take the liberty of recommending myself to her. The failure of the former attempt to send bacon hams to me discouraged me from proposing the attempt again. Yet I should think Mr. Donald could get them to me safely. A dozen or two would last me a year, would be better than any to be had on this side the Atlantic, which, inferior as they are, cost about a guinea apiece . . .

Thomas Jefferson

DOCUMENT 9:

Kitchen Inventory at Monticello Created by James Hemings

Source: "Inventory of Kitchen Utincils,"
Thomas Jefferson Papers, Series 1, General
Correspondence, 1651–1827, Library of Congress,
Manuscript Division.

While serving as a diplomat in Paris, Thomas Jefferson was accompanied by his Virginia slaves Sally Hemings and James Hemings. Sally became Jefferson's mistress, and James became his cook. Jefferson later recalled having gone to "great expence" to have Hemings "taught the art of cookery, desiring to befriend him, and to require from him as little in return as possible." In order to be certain that he would perpetually benefit from his investment in Hemings's French culinary training, Jefferson convinced Hemings not to seize his freedom in Paris, where slavery was illegal, but to return with him to Virginia and to train another enslaved cook. In exchange, Jefferson agreed to free Hemings, a promise he kept. Tragically, several years after his manumission, Hemings committed suicide. This document is Hemings's 1796 inventory of Jefferson's well-equipped kitchen at his home of Monticello.

Inventory of Kitchen Utincils

19 Copper Stew pans—19 Covers
6 Small Sauce pans
3 Copper Baking Moulds
2 Small preserving pans
2 Large—Ditto
2 Copper Fish kettles
2 Copper Brazing pans
2 Round Large—Ditto
2 Iron Stew pans
2 Large Boiling kettles tin'd inside
1 Large Brass—Ditto
12 pewter water Dishes
12—plates
3 Tin Coffie pots
8 Tin Dish Covers
2 frying pans of Iron & one of Copper
4 Round Baking Copper Sheets tin'd
4 Square Copper Ditto untin'd
1 Copper Boiler
1 Copper tea kettle 1 Iron Ditto
2 Small Copper Baking pans
1 Turkish Bonnet Baking mould
3 Waffel Irons
2 Grid Irons
2 Spits—1 Jack—3 Cleavers—2 hold fasts

3 Copper Laidles—4 Copper Spoons—1 Basing Spoon
3 Copper Skimmers—2 Cast Iron Bakers
2 pair Tongs—2 Shovels—1 poker—1 Bake Shovel
2 Large Iron pots—2 Dutch ovens
1 Iron Chaffing Dish,—21 Small Copper Baking moulds
2 Gelly moulds—2 Treising moulds
1 Butter Tin kettle—2 Culinders—1 tin 1 of pewter
1 Brass Culinder 2 Graters—1 old Copper fish kettle
9 wooden Spoons—3 past cuting moulds
1 Brass pistle & mortar—1 Marble Ditto
2 wooden paste Rolers—2 Chopping Knives
6 Iron Crevets—3 tin tart moulds—5 Kitchen apperns
1 old Brass Kettle—1 Iron Candle stick
2 Brass Chaffing Dishes

DOCUMENT 10:

In a Letter to James Monroe, James Madison Reacts to Diplomatic Scandal over Dining Etiquette

Source: Gaillard Hunt, ed. *The Writings of James Madison, Comprising His Public Papers and His Private Correspondence* (New York: G. P. Putnam's Sons, 1900), 118–21.

At an 1803 state dinner given for British diplomat Anthony Merry and his wife, Elizabeth Merry, Thomas Jefferson offended the minister and his wife by his failure to observe conventional dining etiquette. Tradition dictated that Jefferson should have escorted Mrs. Merry, the highest-ranking woman in attendance, to the dining room. He instead offered his arm to Dolley Madison, the wife of his secretary of state. Upon reaching the dining room, Jefferson allowed his guests to seat themselves "pell-mell" in the order they arrived rather than assigning seats based on status. Jefferson claimed that seating based upon rank was not in keeping with the values of the young nation, proclaiming, "When brought together in society, all are perfectly equal, whether foreign or domestic, titled or untitled, in or out of office." The Merrys, however, perceived this practice as a deliberate slight against them, and the events of the dinner compounded strained diplomatic relations between the two countries.

Washington Feby 16. 1804
Dear Sir

In a private letter by Mr. Baring I gave you a detail of what had passed here on the subject of *etiquete. I had hoped that no farther jars would have ensued as I still hope that the good sense of the British government respecting the right of the government here to fix its rules of intercourse and the sentiments and manners of the country to which they ought to be adapted will give the proper instructions for preventing like incidents in future. In the mean time a fresh circumstance has taken place which calls for explanation.*

The President desirous of *keeping open for cordial civilities* whatever channels the *scruples of M. Merry* might not have *closed asked me* what these were *understood to be* and particularly whether he would *come and take friendly* and *familiar dinners with him I* undertook to *feel his pulse* thro' some *hand that would do it* the least *impropriety.* From the information *obtained I inferred* that an *invitation* would be readily *accepted* and with the *less doubt* as *he had dined with me* (his *lady declining) after* the *offence originally taken. The invitation was accordingly sent* and terminated *in the note from him to me & my answer herewith inclosed. I* need not comment on this *display* of *diplomatic* superstition, truly extraordinary in *this age and country.* We are willing to refer it to the *personal character of a man* accustomed to *see importance in such trifles* and over *cautious* against displeasing *his government* by *surrendering* the *minutest of his or its pretentions.* What we *apprehend is* that with these causes may be mingled a *jealousy of our disposition toward England* and that the mortifications which *he has inflicted on himself* are to be set *down to that account.* In fact it is known that this *jealousy* particularly *since the final adjustment with France* exists or is *affected in a high degree* and will doubtless give its *colour to the correspondence of the legation* with *its government.* To apply an *antidote to this poison* will require *your vigilant and prudent attention.* It can scarcely be believed that the British Govt will not at once see the *folly commited by its representative* especially in the last *scene of the farce* and that it will set *him to right in that respect.* But it may *listen* with a different *ear to suggestions* that the U. S. having now *less need of* the *friendship of Britain* may be yielding to a *latent enmity toward her.* The best of all proofs to the *contrary would* be the *confidential communica[tion]s* you possess, if it were not an improper condescension to disclose them for such a purpose. Next to that is the tenor of our measures, and the dictates of our obvious policy; on an appeal to both of which you may found the strongest assurances that the Govt. of the U. S. is sincerely and anxiously disposed to cultivate harmony between the two Nations. The President wishes you to *lose no opportunity and* to *spare* no *pains* that may be necessary to *satisfy the British* Administration *on this head* and to *prevent or efface* any *different impressions* which may be *transmitted from hence.*

I collect that the *cavil at the pele mele here established* turns much on the alledged *degradation* of *ministers* and *envoies to a level with chargés d'affaires.* The truth is, and I have so *told Merry* that this is not the idea; That the President did not mean to decide any thing as to their comparative grades or importance; that these would be *estimated as heretofore;* that among themselves they might fix their own ceremonies, and that even at the *presidents table they might seat themselves* in any *subordination they pleased.* All he meant was that no seats were to be designated for them, nor the order in which they might happen to sit to be any criterion of the respect paid to their respective commissions or Countries. On public occasions, such as Inaugural speech &c. the Heads of Depts. with foreign Ministers, and others invited on the part of the Govt. would be in the same pêle mêle within the space assigned them. It may not be remiss to recollect that under the Old Congress, as I understand, and even in the ceremonies attending the introduction of the new Govt. the foreign ministers were placed according to the order in which their Govts. acknowledged by Treaties the Independence of the U. States. In this point of view the pêle mêle is favorable both to G. B. and to Spain.

I have, I believe already told you that the President has discontinued the *handing first to* the *table* the *wife of a head of department* applying the general *rule of pele mele to that* as *to other cases.*

The Marquis d' Yrujo joined with *Merry in refusing an invitation* from the *President & has* throughout *made a common cause with him* not however approving all the grounds taken by the latter. His case is indeed different and not a little awkward; having acquiesced for nearly three years in the practice agst. which he now revolts. *Pichon* being *a charge only* was *not invited* into the *pretentions of the two plenipotentiarys.* He blames their *contumacy but* I find *he has reported* the *affair to his government* which is not likely to *patronise* the *cause of Merry* & *Yrujo.*

Thornton has *also declined an invitation from the president.* This shews that *he unites* without necessity *with Merry. He has* latterly expressed much *jealousy of our views* founded on *little and unmeaning circumstances.*

The *manners* of *Mistress Merry disgust* both *sexes* and *all parties.* I have time to add only my affecte. respects. . . .

James Madison

CHAPTER 4

Nineteenth-Century
Expansion

Republicanism was a valued concept in the years following the ratification of the US Constitution, and citizens of the newly independent nation were encouraged to participate in civic life. Though women still could not vote or sign legal contracts, they were viewed as educators of the next generation of Americans. The idea of republican motherhood charged women with maintaining home life, raising children, and inculcating in them values like prudence and hard work. Some women looked to reformers like Lydia Maria Child—whose 1832 book *The American Frugal Housewife* is excerpted in the first document in this chapter—for guidance about stretching their food and providing for their families in the expanding but sometimes unstable economy.

The United States grew considerably during the nineteenth century, beginning with the Louisiana Purchase of 1804, which doubled the size of the young republic. Americans began for the first time moving beyond the Appalachian Mountains in large numbers to settle in places like the Ohio River valley. The addition of Texas in 1845 and a large part of Mexico's territory after the Mexican War expanded US holdings all the way to the Pacific Ocean. The construction of new roads, canals, and railroads facilitated trade between the states. Acquisition of vast territory encouraged western settlement but also increased tensions with Native American people who occupied these lands. Westward migrants encountered unfamiliar foodways, such as those of the Pueblo in New Mexico. Three generations of Laguna Pueblo women are shown in document 5 using traditional techniques to process maize. Migrants of European descent who traveled to the Southwest also encountered a vibrant mestizo cuisine that combined plants from the Native American larder, such as chili and corn, with ingredients like wheat and domesticated animals that had been introduced to the region by the Spanish. As other documents in this chapter reveal, homesteaders who headed west packed preserved food but often had to forage or rely on trade with natives to survive the long journey. Meanwhile, cowboys roaming the open land learned to cook simple meals, augmented by increasingly available canned goods.

On the East Coast, immigrants from Europe entered the United States seeking jobs in factories. On the West Coast, Chinese immigrants were hired to help build railroad lines through some of the most forbidding terrain in North America. Mostly men, these immigrants were often isolated and maintained their indigenous foodways by cooking their own meals while laying steel tracks across the land. In cities like San Francisco, Chinese immigrants lived in ethnic communities with restaurants that catered to the tastes of home. The presence of the Chinese came to be resented by the latter part of the century, culminating in the Chinese Exclusion Act of 1882. As demonstrated in document 4, the unfamiliar foodways of the Chinese were a focal point for some nativists who preferred not to see them settle permanently in the United States.

DOCUMENT 1:

Lydia Maria Child Advises American Women, 1832

Source: Lydia Maria Child, *The American Frugal Housewife* (1832).

As the economy expanded during the market revolution, labor became increasingly commoditized through industrialization. Some unmarried women found work outside of the home in textile factories or as domestic laborers, while other women took in sewing or laundry to help make ends meet. However, white women were viewed primarily as homemakers, and their work as cooks, cleaners, and seamstresses for their families went largely uncalculated by the emerging market economy. Politics and public life were the realm of men, while women managed the

domestic sphere. A woman looking for counsel on feed-
ing her children and other issues related to housekeeping
could turn to The American Frugal Housewife, *which*
promoted thrift and quoted Benjamin Franklin, who had
warned that "a fat kitchen maketh a lean will." Originally
published in 1829, the popular volume had gone through
multiple editions by 1832, the version excerpted here.

The true economy of housekeeping is simply the art of gathering up all the fragments, so that nothing be lost. I mean fragments of time, as well as materials. Nothing should be thrown away so long as it is possible to make any use of it, however trifling that use may be; and whatever be the size of a family, every member should be employed either in earning or saving money.

"Time is money." For this reason, cheap as stockings are, it is good economy to knit them. Cotton and woollen yarn are both cheap; hose that are knit wear twice as long as woven ones; and they can be done at odd minutes of time, which would not be otherwise employed. Where there are children, or aged people, it is sufficient to recommend knitting, that it is an employment.

In the country, where grain is raised, it is a good plan to teach children to prepare and braid straw for their own bonnets, and their brothers' hats.

Where turkeys and geese are kept, handsome feather fans may as well be made by the younger members of a family, as to be bought. The sooner children are taught to turn their faculties to some account, the better for them and for their parents. . . .

The writer has no apology to offer for this cheap little book of economical hints, except her deep conviction that such a book is needed. In this case, renown is out of the question, and ridicule is matter of indifference.

The information conveyed is of a common kind; but it is such as the majority of young housekeepers do not possess, and such as they cannot obtain from cookery books. Books of this kind have usually been written for the wealthy: I have written for the poor. . . . I have attempted to teach how money can be saved, not how it can be enjoyed. If any persons think some of the maxims too rigidly economical, let them inquire how the largest fortunes among us have been made. They will find thousands and millions have been accumulated by a scrupulous attention to sums "infinitely more minute than sixty cents."

Odd Scraps for the Economical.

If you would avoid waste in your family, attend to the following rules, and do not despise them because they appear so unimportant: "many a little makes a mickle."

Look frequently to the pails, to see that nothing is thrown to the pigs which should have been in the grease-pot.

Look to the grease-pot, and see that nothing is there which might have served to nourish your own family, or a poorer one.

See that the beef and pork are always under brine; and that the brine is sweet and clean.

See that the vegetables are neither sprouting nor decaying: if they are so, remove them to a drier place, and spread them.

Examine preserves, to see that they are not contracting mould; and your pickles, to see that they are not growing soft and tasteless.

As far as it is possible, have bits of bread eaten up before they become hard. Spread those that are not eaten, and let them dry, to be pounded for puddings, or soaked for brewis. Brewis is made of crusts and dry pieces of bread, soaked a good while in hot milk, mashed up, and salted, and buttered like toast. Above all, do not let crusts accumulate in such quantities that they cannot be used. With proper care, there is no need of losing a particle of bread, even in the hottest weather.

Make your own bread and cake. Some people think it is just as cheap to buy of the baker and confectioner; but it is not half as cheap. True, it is more convenient; and therefore the rich are justifiable in employing them; but those who are under the necessity of being economical, should make convenience a secondary object. . . .

Eggs will keep almost any length of time in lime-water properly prepared. One pint of coarse salt, and one pint of unslacked lime, to a pailful of water. If there be too much lime, it will eat the shells from the eggs; and if there be a single egg cracked, it will spoil the whole. . . .

New England rum, constantly used to wash the hair, keeps it very clean, and free from disease, and promotes its growth a great deal more than Macassar oil. Brandy is very strengthening to the roots of the hair; but it has a hot, drying tendency, which N.E. rum has not.

There should always be a heavy stone on the top of your pork, to keep it down. This stone is an excellent place to keep a bit of fresh meat in the summer, when you are afraid of its spoiling.

Have all the good bits of vegetables and meat collected after dinner, and minced before they are set away; that they may be in readiness to make a little savoury mince meat for supper or breakfast. Take the skins off your potatoes before they grow cold.

Green tea is excellent to restore rusty silk. It should be boiled in iron, nearly a cup full to three quarts. The silk should not be wrung, and should be ironed damp.

DOCUMENT 2:

Memoir of a Wagon Train to California, 1849

Source: L. Dow Stephens, *Life Sketches of a Jayhawker of '49* (San Jose: Nolta Brothers, 1916), 7–22 (excerpts).

By the 1840s, many Americans, including President Polk, believed that it was the country's Manifest Destiny to expand to the Pacific Ocean. With the acquisition of California through the Mexican War, intrepid settlers packed up their belongings in covered wagons to start new lives in the West. After the gold rush in the Sierra Nevada Mountains, the lure of California took on almost a mythic quality, enticing professional and amateur miners to gamble for a mineral fortune. Traveling to California by land, however, was fraught with dangers, including wild animals, weather events, and hostile Native Americans. Perhaps the biggest threat of all was that of starvation, which was tragically illustrated by the Donner party's desperate turn to cannibalism in 1846. As a young man in his early twenties, Lorenzo Dow Stephens joined a group heading for California in 1849. Along the way he encountered cattle drives, prospectors, and Mormons, but food

was a constant theme as he foraged, traded, and won-
dered at times if he might starve to death.

On March 28, 1849, the expedition started on its long and too many fatal journey. The outfits generally consisted of three to four yoke of oxen, good strong wagons well loaded with provisions, bedding and clothing. In fact we found later that we were too heavily loaded. Let me say here that the hardest pull we had was the leave-taking. We were leaving behind home, all that was near and dear, all the friends among whom our youthful days were spent. In fact I never realized how hard a pull it was until I came to bid good-bye and started to drive away. I never felt so much like backing out of any undertaking as I did then, but I had too much pride to stand laughter, so the reins were gathered up and the expedition moved.

Iowa, at this time, was very sparsely settled. Farm houses were twenty miles and more apart, and we found here and there villages of cheap unpainted houses. We found game in plenty, consisting chiefly of deer, wild turkeys and prairie chickens. When we reached the Missouri River at Council Bluff, we travelled down the river to Traders' Point, a distance of ten or twelve miles. Here we remained for a week, waiting for the grass to get a good start, arranging for a larger expedition. This point was the end of the Settlements, and further on lay the Indian country. . . .

Somewhere in the Western part of Iowa we passed the grave of the Indian Chief, Black Hawk, of Black Hawk War fame. It was near the bank of a small stream, the name of which I've forgotten. We had a little mishap here in rafting the stream. Our raft was going along nicely when in some way the wagon went to the bottom of the river, out of sight. The stream was sluggish, and we didn't have much difficulty in fishing the wagon out. Fortunately the load had been transferred to another wagon, but we did have one load damaged on another occasion when the wagon turned over crossing a stream. This was quite serious, as three barrels of hard bread were entirely ruined. . . .

Many amusing incidents happened every day hardly worth recording. In the evenings, many times friendly Indians came into camp numbering thirty or forty. Sometimes they brought things to trade, and then again they begged for food. Indians seem to be hungry at all times. One evening, while the Indians were in camp, a man with false teeth went up to them smiling a most pleasing smile and showing his beautiful white teeth. He would turn around, grin at them again, this time showing his gums. He had only to repeat this several times when the Indians would back away, walk off, and in a few moments start into a trot until they were out of sight. They thought, of course, that the man was an evil spirit, but I have often wondered just what they did think.

Along the Platte River we found the corpses of Indians, well wrapped in bark and tied to the limbs of trees with bark. This was the custom of the Pawnees, but after we got further on the plains there were no trees, in fact no trees for five hundred miles. So we had no fuel, and had to use the buffalo chips, which, if dry, made a very hot fire. Just before camping time we each of us took a sack, scattered out and came back to camp with sacks full, having a generous supply for cooking our supper and breakfast. But if the rain came on, our much prized chips would not burn at all, and we had to be content with hard tack and raw bacon, and no hot coffee for breakfast. . . .

We were very much over-loaded and in consequence the cattle could not stand the strain, and grew weaker day by day. So hundreds of pounds of the finest bacon, beans, flour and sugar were left on the wayside. The bacon was piled like cordwood, and some of the men poured turpentine on the provisions and set fire to them, so the Indians couldn't eat them. Some men seem to be born mean, but to me such meanness was despicable.

At this juncture we were approaching Salt Lake City, so three of us decided to forge ahead of the train. When we reached the first bench or table land we saw spread out before us the city itself, and in the greater distance the Great Lake. When we reached the first little farm our attention was attracted to the garden, full of vegetables of all kinds. How our mouths watered at this welcome sight. We approached the house, asked for accommodations. They made excuses about sleeping quarters, but that didn't trouble us, as we could sleep anywhere out of doors, if one could just have a meal or so. We kept our eyes on the garden, and were willing and glad to help in the preparation of the vegetables. No one knows how willing we were to pod the peas. We had green corn, peas and other vegetables, something we had longed and starved for four months. Never before or since have I tasted anything that was so good, and we ate and ate until we could eat no more, and only felt sorry that our capacity was so limited.

Our train arrived the same day and we were soon surrounded by the Mormons, principally women enquiring for tea, and if we had any to sell. They seemed to be as much starved for tea as we were for vegetables. We wouldn't sell tea, but we said we would trade for vegetables. Tea was three dollars a pound, and we could get vegetables a week for a pound of tea. Some of the women said they had not tasted tea for two years past. They were also short of groceries and wearing apparel. Many women were entirely barefooted, and many scantily dressed. All the clothes had been practically worn out, as there had been no supplies brought in for two years, consequently many of them were greatly in need of the luxuries of life. They had seeds and plenty of cattle with them, so they were well provided with the substantials, all having good gardens, beef, milk and butter. . . .

On one occasion we had gone five days without water, but through a kind Providence on the third night a snow came. About two or three inches fell, but before the ground was barely covered we were all out gathering the snow to melt, and before the storm had passed we had ample supply for ourselves and oxen. No doubt this is what saved many of us, for we never reached water for two days more. It became a cause of anxiety, whether we would ever reach the next watering place or not. It became the custom toward the last to send out men to prospect for water, and if water was found a smoke was made, as in this desert country smoke could be seen a great distance.

From day to day our cattle became weaker and weaker, and our provisions were getting low. So we were put on short allowance. Finally the teams could pull no further, many had already died, so the wagons were abandoned and pack saddles made on the oxen.

On Christmas day, 1849, we were all busy making pack saddles, and cooking the scanty supply of flour into little biscuits, or crackers, as they were perfectly hard. We were divided into twos, from eight men to two men mess, and each one had his share allotted to him. We had a half dozen of the little crackers, about three or four spoonfuls of rice, and about as much dried apples, and this ended the bill of fare, which must last until we reached settlements.

California seemed a long way off. We did not know where we were, but I know we were much further off than we realized. The proposition now became a single one, for we just had to subsist on the oxen, and they had become so poor there was little or no nourishment in their flesh, as they were dying then from starvation.

Speaking of thirst, there is no punishment that has any comparison. It is the most agonizing suffering possible and the feeling is indescribable. Our tongues would be swollen, our lips crack, and a crust would form on our tongue and roof of mouth that could not be removed. The body seemed to be dried through and through, and there wouldn't be a drop of moisture in the mouth. . . .

So day by day we pursued our way, our cattle and ourselves growing weaker and weaker. The outlook was gloomy, and often when we killed a steer we looked forward to the marrow found in the bones. But in breaking the bones often there would be nothing there but a little bloody substance, and I suppose our bones were much in the same condition, as we had becomes as starved as they were.

I remember one incident relating to this and that was the case of Captain Asa Haines. He was quite elderly compared with the rest of us, probably sixty years of age. He would remark, "Boys, if I only had the corn that my hogs at home are rooting in the mud I would consider it the greatest luxury imaginable," and then would cry like a baby. A few days later he said to us, "Boys, I feel that I can't go any further and I'll have to leave you." I knew then that he would die soon, and told my mess-mate, Bill Rude, that Captain Haines would not live until morning. We had each saved two or three of our little biscuits and a couple of spoonfuls of rice. I told Bill I was willing to give all I had to Asa Haines if he would. So we took the last morsel we had saved, made a kind of stew of it and carried this to Haines. He said, "Boys, you have saved my life," and we knew we had. It did us more good, yes ten times over, than if we had eaten it ourselves.

DOCUMENT 3:

Cowboys Eating on the Range

Source: Library of Congress, Prints and
Photographs Division, reproduction
#LC-USZ62–16318.

Cowboys who herded cattle lived a rustic existence moving cows from one region to another by way of paths like the Chisholm Trail that ran from Texas to Kansas. By the 1870s, ranchers could use railroads to get their cattle to the marketplace more efficiently, and the need for cowboys to drive herds began to decline. The use of barbed wire by the end of the century signaled the end of the open range as landowners marked off their territory. However, during the days of long cattle drives, cowboys usually worked in groups and depended on a chuck wagon, like the one pictured below, to carry provisions for meals.

Document 3

DOCUMENT 4:

Song about John Chinaman, 1850s

Source: D. E. Appleton, ed., *The California Songster* (San Francisco: Noisy Carriers Book and Stationery Co., 1855), 44.

The name "John Chinaman" was a denigrating way of referring to Chinese immigrants in the nineteenth century. Chinese laborers were hired to work on the railroads, and through their arduous efforts some of the most difficult and dangerous portions of track were laid across the terrain of the western United States. However, the immigrants were often viewed with disdain, and there was a perception that they were entering the country in large numbers even though most of the immigrants were single males and many eventually returned to their families in China. Chinese workers were portrayed often as conniving and untrustworthy in popular poems and songs, like Bret Harte's "The Heathen Chinee" from 1870, which tells the story of a Chinese man who pretends not to understand a card game but in reality is a cheating hustler. The Chinese were considered to be unable to assimilate because much of their culture was very foreign and largely misunderstood in the West. In the song "John Chinaman" below, the unknown writer laments the Chinese immigrants' failure to acculturate and points to the diet of the Chinese as particularly offensive.

John Chinaman, John Chinaman
But five short years ago,
I welcomed you from Canton, John—
But wish I hadn't though;
For then I thought you honest, John,
Not dreaming but you'd make
A citizen as useful, John

As any in the state.
I thought you'd open wide your ports
And let our merchants in
To barter for their crapes and teas,
Their wares of wood and tin.
I thought you'd cut your queue off, John,
And don a Yankee coat,
And a collar high you'd raise, John,
Around your dusky throat.
I imagined that the truth, John,
You'd speak when under oath,
But I find you'll lie and steal too—
Yes, John, you're up to both.
I thought of rats and puppies, John,
You'd eaten your last fill;
But on such slimy pot-pies, John,
I'm told you dinner still.
Oh, John, I've been deceived in you,
And all your thieving clan,
For our gold is all you're after, John,
To get it as you can.

DOCUMENT 5:

Laguna Pueblo Women Grinding Corn

Source: Library of Congress, Prints and
Photographs Division, reproduction
#LC-USZ62–59798.

When Mexico gained independence from Spain in 1821, the area now known as New Mexico was home to around ten thousand Pueblo Indians. Following the Mexican War, that area was incorporated into the United States. Corn was a fundamental part of the Pueblo diet and was central to their creation narrative in which the Corn Mother was an important giver of life. Annual corn dances in

Document 5

the summer honor indigenous religious figures as well as Christian saints. In the image above, traditional culinary techniques are practiced by three generations of Laguna Pueblo women.

DOCUMENT 6:

Rose Wilder Lane's Memoir of Life in the West, 1880s

Source: Autobiographical sketch of Rose Wilder Lane, Library of Congress, American Life Histories: Manuscripts from the Federal Writer's Project, 1936–1940.

The Homestead Act, which was passed by Congress in 1862, promised title on 160 acres of land to families who established farms within five years. This law helped populate western lands with family farms as hundreds of thousands of homesteaders took advantage of this offer by the early twentieth century. The economic climate of the late nineteenth century, however, was not always friendly to small farmers. Panics and depressions occurred in the 1870s and 1890s, and prices on staple crops suffered. The Populist movement grew out of the desire to ameliorate the economic hardships facing many farmers, especially those in the plains and the West. In the memoir below, Rose Wilder Lane recalls the difficulties her family encountered while trying to establish a family farm in the Dakotas, difficulties that prompted their move to Missouri. Her mother, Laura Ingalls Wilder, immortalized the Wilder family's experiences in the West in the children's series Little House on the Prairie. As Rose recalled, it often took ingenuity as well as hard work and cooperation just to feed a family of homesteaders. She writes about the depression following the crash of 1893 from the perspective of the depression of the 1930s.

I was born in Dakota Territory, in a . . . shanty, forty-nine years ago come next December. It doesn't seem possible. My father's people were English . . . [and] his ancestors came to America in 1630 and, farming progressively westward, reached Minnesota during my father's boyhood. Naturally, he took a homestead farther west. My mother's ancestors were Scotch and French; her father's cousin was John J. Ingalls, who, "lie a lonely crane, swore and swore and stalked the Kansas plain." She is Laura Ingalls Wilder, writer of books for children.

Conditions had changed when I was born; there was no more free land. Of course, there never had been free land. It was a saying in the Dakotas that the Government bet a quarter section against fifteen dollars and five years' hard work that the land would starve a man out in less than five years. My father won the bet. It took seven successive years of complete crop failure, with work, weather and sickness that wrecked his health permanently, and interest rates of 36 per cent on money borrowed to buy food, to dislodge us from that land. I was then seven years old. . . .

We reached the Missouri at Yankton, in a string of other covered wagons. The ferryman took them one by one, across the wide yellow river. I sat between my parents in the wagon on the river bank, anxiously hoping to get across before dark. Suddenly the rear end of the wagon jumped into the air and came down with a terrific crash. My mother seized the lines; my father leaped over the wheel and in desperate haste tied the wagon to the ground, with ropes to picket pins deeply driven in. The loaded wagon kept lifting off the ground, straining at the ropes; they creaked and stretched, but held. They kept [the] wagon and horses from being blown into the river.

Looking around the edge of the wagon covers I saw the whole earth behind us billowing to the sky. There was something savage and terrifying in the howling yellow swallowing the sky. The color came, I now suppose, from the sunset.

"Well, that's our last sight of Dakota," my mother said. "We're getting out with a team and wagon; that's more than a lot can say," my father answered cheerfully.

This was during the panic of [18]93. The whole Middle West was shaken loose and moving. We joined long wagon trains moving south; we met hundreds of wagons going north; the roads east and west were crawling lines of families traveling under canvas, looking for work, for another foothold somewhere on the land. By the fires in the camps I heard talk about Coxey's army, 60,000 men, marching on Washington; Federal troops had been called out. The country was ruined, the whole world was ruined; nothing like this had ever happened before. There was no hope, but everyone felt the courage of despair. Next morning wagons went on to the north, from which we had been driven, and we went on toward the south, where those families had not been able to live.

We were not starving. My mother had baked quantities of hardtack for the journey; we had salt meat and beans. My father tried to sell the new—and incredible—asbestos mats that would keep food from burning; no one had ten cents to pay for one, but often he traded for eggs or milk. In Nebraska we found an astoundingly prosperous colony of Russians; we could not talk to them. The Russian women gave us—outright gave us—milk and cream and butter from the abundance of their dairies, and a pan of biscuits. My mouth watered at the sight. And because my mother could not talk to them, and so could not politely refuse these gifts, we had to take them and she to give in exchange some cherished trinket of hers. She had to, because it would have been like taking charity not to make some return. That night we had buttered biscuits.

These Russians had brought from Russia a new kind of wheat— winter wheat, the foundation of future prosperity from the Dakotas to Texas.

Three months after we had ferried across the Missouri, we reached the Ozark hills. It was strange not to hear the wind any more. My parents had great good fortune; with their last hoarded dollar, they were able to buy a piece of poor ridge land, uncleared, with a log cabin and a heavy mortgage on it. My father was an invalid, my mother was a girl in her twenties, I was seven years old.

Good fortune continued. We had hardly moved in to the cabin, when a stranger came pleading for work. His wife and children camped by the road, were starving. We still had a piece of salt pork. The terrible question was, "Dare we risk any of it?" My father did; he offered half of it for a day's work. The stranger was overjoyed. Together they worked from dawn to sunset, putting down trees, sawing and splitting the wood, piling into the wagon all it would hole. Next day my father drove to town with the wood.

It was dark before we heard the wagon coming back. I ran to meet it. It was empty. My father had sold that wood for fifty cents in cash. Delirious, I rushed into the house shouting the news. Fifty cents! My mother cried for joy.

That was the turning point. We lived all winter and kept the camper's family alive till he got a job; he was a hard worker. He and my father cleared land, sold wood, built a log barn. When he moved on, my mother took his place at the cross-cut saw. Next spring a crop was planted; I helped put in the corn, and on the hills I picked green huckleberries to make a pie.

I picked ripe huckleberries, walked a mile and a half to town, and sold them for ten cents a gallon. Blackberries, too. Once I chased a rabbit into a hollow log and barricaded it there with rocks; we had rabbit stew. We were prospering and cheerful. The second summer, my father bought a cow. Then we had milk, and I helped churn; my mother's good butter sold for ten cents a pound. We were paying . . . interest on the mortgage and a yearly bonus for renewal.

That was forty years ago. Rocky Ridge Farm is now 200 acres, in meadow, pasture and field; there are wood lots, but otherwise the land is cleared, and it is clear. The three houses on it have central heating, modern plumbing, electric ranges and refrigerators, garages for three cars. This submarginal farm, in a largely submarginal but comfortably prosperous county, helps support some seven hundred families on relief. They live in miserably small houses and many lack bedsteads on which to put the mattresses, sheets and bedding issued to them. The men on work relief get only twenty cents an hour, only sixteen hours a week. No one bothers now to pick wild berries; it horrifies anybody to think of a child's working three or four hours for ten cents. No farmer's wife sells butter . . . and butterfat brings twenty-six cents. Forty years ago I lived through a world-wide depression; once more I am living through a depression popularly believed to be the worst in history because it is world-wide; this is the ultimate disaster, the depression to end all depressions. On every side I hear that conditions have changed, and that is true. They have.

Meanwhile I have done several things. I have been office clerk, telegrapher, newspaper reporter, feature writer, advertising writer, farmland salesman. I have seen all the United States and something of Canada and the Caribbean; all of Europe except Spain; Turkey, Egypt, Palestine, Syria, Iraq as far east as Bagdad, Georgia, Armenia, Azerbaijan.

. . . Personally, I'm a plump, Middle-Western, Middle-class, middle-aged woman, with white hair and simple tastes. I like buttered popcorn, salted peanuts, bread-and-milk. I am, however, a marvelous cook of foods for others to eat. I like to see people eat my cooking. I love mountains, the sea—all of the seas except the Atlantic, a rather dull ocean—and Tschaikovsky and Epstein and the Italian primitives. I like Arabic architecture and the Moslem way of life. I am mad about Kansas skies, Cedar Rapids by night, Iowa City any time, Miami Beach, San Francisco, and all American boys about fifteen years old playing basketball. At the moment I don't think of anything I heartily dislike, but I can't understand sport pages, nor what makes [a] radio work, nor why people like to look at people who write fiction.

CHAPTER 5

Foodways during Enslavement and War

The expansion of US territory led to the spread of slavery in the early nineteenth century. Following Eli Whitney's invention of the cotton gin, large-scale cotton farming became quite profitable, and plantations stretched from the Carolinas and Georgia all the way to eastern Texas. However, the proliferation of the slave system became an increasingly bitter point of debate since states north of Maryland had begun a process of gradual emancipation beginning in the late 1700s. As abolitionists became more vocal and defenders of the institution more resolute, disputes over the issue of slavery became heated. When new states entered the union crises emerged over whether or not slavery would be permitted within their individual borders. A key tool for abolitionists to argue against slavery on moral grounds was the firsthand testimony of the enslaved. Slave narratives described all aspects of the lives of those who had been held in bondage. In their autobiographies, which are excerpted in documents 2 and 3, respectively, Frederick Douglass and Harriet Jacobs often used food and the memory of hunger as potent illustrations of their oppression. On the other hand, as document 1 reveals, cookbooks like *The Virginia Housewife* demonstrated that African influences, such as the use of okra and a preference for highly seasoned food, had become chief characteristics of southern foodways.

Once the Civil War erupted in 1861, provisioning the two armies became a paramount task for the Union and the Confederacy. Receiving care packages from home was a joy in the early years of the war and became indispensable as the war dragged on and the South, especially, struggled to provide for its soldiers. Deprivation among civilians became so acute that bread riots exploded in Georgia, Alabama, North

Carolina, and Virginia. The patience of women who had been asked to sacrifice for the war was running thin as they strove to fill the bellies of their children who were still at home. Interestingly, it was during the turmoil of war in 1863 that President Abraham Lincoln proclaimed that the country should set aside a day in November in order to "solemnly, reverently and gratefully" offer thanksgiving. Lincoln's proclamation of a national day of "Thanksgiving" appears in document 6. In the tumult that followed the war years, books like Annabella Hill's cookbook offered advice and recipes for southern women who were managing kitchens in which enslaved cooks were now absent.

DOCUMENT 1:

Recipes and Advice for Southern Cooks, 1824

Source: Mary Randolph, *The Virginia Housewife* (Washington, DC: Davis and Force, 1824).

Mrs. Mary Randolph had a reputation as a good cook and welcoming hostess in Richmond, Virginia, where she ran a boardinghouse with her husband, David Meade Randolph. Many scholars consider her book, The Virginia Housewife, *to be the first regional cookbook published in the United States. The volume proved to be popular when it first came out in 1824, and it went through many editions until at least 1860. Randolph offered detailed advice on all aspects of cooking and kitchen management, including baking bread and biscuits, making jelly and preserves, dressing a salad, boiling potatoes, curing bacon and herring, making sausage, butchering and dressing cuts of meat, and even making cordials and beer. Instructions for undertaking tasks like drying herbs, making soap, and polishing silver helped new housewives. The text illustrates the variety of foreign influences in antebellum southern cooking. Ingredients like okra were from Africa, while other dishes like the pepper pot were West Indian.*

INTRODUCTION

Management is an art that may be acquired by every woman of good sense and tolerable memory. If, unfortunately, she has been bred in a family where domestic business is the work of chance, she will have many difficulties to encounter; but a determined resolution to obtain this valuable knowledge, will enable her to surmount all obstacles. She must begin the day with an early breakfast, requiring each person to be in readiness to take their seats when the muffins, buckwheat cakes, &c. are placed on the table. This looks social and comfortable. When the family breakfast by detachments, the table remains a tedious time; the servants are kept from their morning's meal, and a complete derangement takes place in the whole business of the day. No work can be done till breakfast is finished. The Virginia ladies, who are proverbially good managers, employ themselves, while their servants are eating, in washing the cups, glasses, &c.; arranging the cruets, the mustard, salt-sellers, pickle vases, and all the apparatus for the dinner table. This occupies but a short time, and the lady has the satisfaction of knowing that they are in much better order than they would be if left to the servants. It also relieves her from the trouble of seeing the dinner table prepared, which should be done every day with the same scrupulous regard to exact neatness and method, as if a grand company was expected. When the servant is required to do this daily, he soon gets into the habit of doing it well; and his mistress having made arrangements for him in the morning, there is no fear of bustle and confusion in running after things that may be called for during the hour of dinner. When the kitchen breakfast is over, and the cook has put all things in their proper places, the mistress should go in to give her orders. Let all the articles intended for the dinner, pass in review before her: have the butter, sugar, flour, meal, lard, given out in proper quantities; the catsup, spice, wine, whatever may be wanted for each dish, measured to the cook. The mistress must tax her own memory with all this: we have no right to expect slaves or hired servants to be more attentive to our interest than we ourselves are: they will never recollect these little articles until they are going to use them; the mistress must then be called out, and thus have the horrible drudgery of keeping house all day, when one hour devoted to it in the morning, would release her from trouble until the next day. There is economy as well as comfort in a regular mode of doing business. When the mistress gives out every thing, there is no waste; but if temptation be thrown in the way of subordinates, not many will have power to resist it; besides, it is an immoral act to place them in a situation which we pray to be exempt from ourselves.

The prosperity and happiness of a family depend greatly on the order and regularity established in it. The husband, who can ask a friend to partake of his dinner in full confidence of finding his wife unruffled by the petty vexations attendant on the neglect of household duties—who can usher his guest into the dining-room assured of seeing that methodical nicety which is the essence of true elegance,—will feel pride and exultation in the possession of a companion, who gives to his home charms that gratify every wish of his soul, and render the haunts of dissipation hateful to him. The sons bred in such a family will be moral men, of steady habits; and the daughters, if the mother shall have performed the duties of a parent in the superintendence of their education, as faithfully as she has done those of a wife, will each be a treasure to her husband; and being formed on the model of an exemplary mother, will use the same means for securing the happiness of her own family, which she has seen successfully practised under the paternal roof.

OCHRA SOUP.

Get two double handsful of young ochra, wash and slice it thin, add two onions chopped fine, put it into a gallon of water at a very early hour in an earthen pipkin, or very nice iron pot; it must be kept steadily simmering, but not boiling: put in pepper and salt. At 12 o'clock, put in a handful of Lima beans; at half-past one o'clock, add three young cimlins cleaned and cut in small pieces, a fowl, or knuckle of veal, a bit of bacon or pork that has been boiled, and six tomatos, with the skin taken off; when nearly done, thicken with a spoonful of butter, mixed with one of flour. Have rice boiled to eat with it.

OCHRA AND TOMATOS.

Take an equal quantity of each, let the ochra be young, slice it, and skin the tomatos; put them into a pan without water, add a lump of butter, an onion chopped fine, some pepper and salt, and stew them one hour.

GUMBO—A WEST INDIA DISH.

Gather young pods of ochra, wash them clean, and put them in a pan with a little water, salt and pepper, stew them till tender, and serve them with melted butter. They are very nutritious, and easy of digestion.

PEPPER POT.

Boil two or three pounds of tripe, cut it in pieces, and put it on the fire with a knuckle of veal, and a sufficient quantity of water; part of a pod of pepper, a little spice, sweet herbs according to your taste, salt, and some dumplins; stew it till tender, and thicken the gravy with butter and flour.

SWEET POTATOS STEWED.

Wash and wipe them, and if they be large, cut them in two lengths; put them at the bottom of a stew pan, lay over some slices of boiled ham; and on that, one or two chickens cut up with pepper, salt, and a bundle of herbs; pour in some water, and stew them till done, then take out the herbs, serve the stew in a deep dish—thicken the gravy, and pour over it.

SWEET POTATO PUDDING.

Boil one pound of sweet potatos very tender, rub them while hot through a colander; add six eggs well beaten, three quarters of a pound of powdered sugar, three quarters of butter, and some grated nutmeg and lemon peel, with a glass of brandy; put a paste in the dish, and when the pudding is done, sprinkle the top with sugar, and cover it with bits of citron. Irish potato pudding is made in the same manner, but is not so good.

Frederick Douglass Recalls Childhood Hunger, 1845

Source: Frederick Douglass, *Narrative of the Life of Frederick Douglass an American Slave Written by Himself* (Boston, 1845).

When his autobiography was published in 1845, Frederick Douglass became a well-known figure in the abolitionist community. He was sought after as a speaker, touring the United States and Great Britain. However, he took a great risk by publishing his life story as an escaped slave who could be recaptured at any time. Ultimately, a benefactor in England paid for his manumission. Perhaps the most eloquent and powerful of the slave narratives, Douglass's memoir indicts the slave system from many angles. Some of the most poignant testimony about his childhood deals with the scarcity of food. The relative availability of food in the various households where he lived also enabled Douglass to portray the relative cruelty or humanity of the masters who owned him.

Colonel Lloyd kept from three to four hundred slaves on his home plantation, and owned a large number more on the neighboring farms belonging to him. The names of the farms nearest to the home plantation were Wye Town and New Design. "Wye Town" was under the overseership of a man named Noah Willis. New Design was under the overseership of a Mr. Townsend. The overseers of these, and all the rest of the farms, numbering over twenty, received advice and direction from the managers of the home plantation. This was the great business place. It was the seat of government for the whole twenty farms. . . .

Here, too, the slaves of all the other farms received their monthly allowance of food, and their yearly clothing. The men and women slaves received, as their monthly allowance of food, eight pounds of pork, or its equivalent in fish, and one bushel of corn meal. Their yearly clothing consisted of two coarse linen shirts, one pair of linen trousers, like the shirts, one jacket, one pair of trousers for winter, made of coarse negro cloth, one pair of stockings, and one pair of shoes; the whole of which could not have cost more than seven dollars. The allowance of the slave children was given to their mothers, or the old women having the care of them. The children unable to work in the field had neither shoes, stockings, jackets, nor trousers, given to them; their clothing consisted of two coarse linen shirts per year. When these failed them, they went naked until the next allowance-day. Children from seven to ten years old, of both sexes, almost naked, might be seen at all seasons of the year. . . .

Colonel Lloyd kept a large and finely cultivated garden, which afforded almost constant employment for four men, besides the chief gardener, (Mr. M'Durmond.) This garden was probably the greatest attraction of the place. During the summer months, people came from far and near—from Baltimore, Easton, and Annapolis—to see it. It abounded in fruits of almost every description, from the hardy apple of the north to the delicate orange of the south. This garden was not the least source of trouble on the plantation. Its excellent fruit was quite a temptation to the hungry swarms of boys, as well as the older slaves, belonging to the colonel, few of whom had the virtue or the vice to resist it. Scarcely a day passed, during the summer, but that some slave had to take the lash for stealing fruit. The colonel had to resort to all kinds of stratagems to keep his slaves out of the garden. The last and most successful one was that of tarring his fence all around; after which, if a slave was caught with any tar upon his person, it was deemed sufficient proof that he had either been into the garden, or had tried to get in. In either case, he was severely whipped by the chief gardener. This plan worked well; the slaves became as fearful of tar as of the lash. They seemed to realize the impossibility of touching *tar* without being defiled.

As to my own treatment while I lived on Colonel Lloyd's plantation, it was very similar to that of the other slave children. I was not old enough to work in the field, and there being little else than field work to do, I had a great deal of leisure time. The most I had to do was to drive up the cows at evening, keep the fowls out of the garden, keep the front yard clean, and run of errands for my old master's daughter, Mrs. Lucretia Auld. The most of my leisure time I spent in helping Master

Daniel Lloyd in finding his birds, after he had shot them. My connection with Master Daniel was of some advantage to me. He became quite attached to me, and was a sort of protector of me. He would not allow the older boys to impose upon me, and would divide his cakes with me.

I was seldom whipped by my old master, and suffered little from any thing else than hunger and cold. I suffered much from hunger, but much more from cold. In hottest summer and coldest winter, I was kept almost naked—no shoes, no stockings, no jacket, no trousers, nothing on but a coarse tow linen shirt, reaching only to my knees. I had no bed. I must have perished with cold, but that, the coldest nights, I used to steal a bag which was used for carrying corn to the mill. I would crawl into this bag, and there sleep on the cold, damp, clay floor, with my head in and feet out. My feet have been so cracked with the frost, that the pen with which I am writing might be laid in the gashes.

We were not regularly allowanced. Our food was coarse corn meal boiled. This was called MUSH. It was put into a large wooden tray or trough, and set down upon the ground. The children were then called, like so many pigs, and like so many pigs they would come and devour the mush; some with oyster-shells, others with pieces of shingle, some with naked hands, and none with spoons. He that ate fastest got most; he that was strongest secured the best place; and few left the trough satisfied. . . .

I lived with Mr. Covey one year. During the first six months, of that year, scarce a week passed without his whipping me. I was seldom free from a sore back. My awkwardness was almost always his excuse for whipping me. We were worked fully up to the point of endurance. Long before day we were up, our horses fed, and by the first approach of day we were off to the field with our hoes and ploughing teams. Mr. Covey gave us enough to eat, but scarce time to eat it. We were often less than five minutes taking our meals. We were often in the field from the first approach of day till its last lingering ray had left us; and at saving-fodder time, midnight often caught us in the field binding blades. . . .

My term of actual service to Mr. Edward Covey ended on Christmas day, 1833. The days between Christmas and New Year's day are allowed as holidays; and, accordingly, we were not required to perform any labor, more than to feed and take care of the stock. This time we regarded as our own, by the grace of our masters; and we therefore used or abused it nearly as we pleased. Those of us who had families at a distance, were generally allowed to spend the whole six days in their society. This time, however, was spent in various ways. The staid, sober, thinking and industrious ones of our number would employ themselves in making corn-brooms, mats, horse-collars, and baskets; and another class of us would spend the time in hunting opossums, hares, and coons. But by far the larger part engaged in such sports and merriments as playing ball, wrestling, running foot-races, fiddling, dancing, and drinking whisky; and this latter mode of spending the time was by far the most agreeable to the feelings of our masters. A slave who would work during the holidays was considered by our masters as scarcely deserving them. He was regarded as one who rejected the favor of his master. It was deemed a disgrace not to get drunk at Christmas; and he was regarded as lazy indeed, who had not provided himself with the necessary means, during the year, to get whisky enough to last him through Christmas. From what I know of the effect of these holidays upon the slave, I believe them to be among the most effective means in the hands of the slaveholder in keeping down the spirit of insurrection. Were the slaveholders at once to abandon this practice, I have not the slightest doubt it would lead to an immediate insurrection among the slaves. These holidays serve as conductors, or safety-valves, to carry off the rebellious spirit of enslaved humanity. But for these, the slave would be forced up to the wildest desperation; and woe betide the slaveholder, the day he ventures to remove or hinder the operation of those conductors! I warn him that, in such an event, a spirit will go forth in their midst, more to be dreaded than the most appalling earthquake.

DOCUMENT 3:

Harriet Jacobs's Memoir, 1861

Source: Harriet Jacobs, *Incidents in the Life of a Slave Girl* (Boston, 1861).

Incidents in the Life of Slave Girl, *one of the relatively few slave narratives written by a woman, recounts Harriet Jacobs's harrowing escape from an abusive master. The book was originally published under the pen name Linda Brent. Jacobs was initially reticent about making her memoir public, but abolitionists like Lydia Maria Child, who edited Jacobs's book, helped persuade her that the particular brutalities suffered by women under enslavement had to come to light. While the cruelty of her master was made plain, Jacobs also carefully rendered the relationship she had with her grandmother, who was a talented cook. Having a cook in the family proved to be important for Jacobs, who was able to supplement her diet with her grandmother's cooking. When Jacobs went into hiding, her grandmother and uncle were able to keep her alive by sneaking food to her.*

I was born a slave; but I never knew it till six years of happy childhood had passed away. My father was a carpenter, and considered so intelligent and skilful in his trade, that, when buildings out of the common line were to be erected, he was sent for from long distances, to be head workman. On condition of paying his mistress two hundred dollars a year, and supporting himself, he was allowed to work at his trade, and manage his own affairs. His strongest wish was to purchase his children; but, though he several times offered his hard earnings for that purpose, he never succeeded. . . . I had also a great treasure in my maternal grandmother, who was a remarkable woman in many respects. She was the daughter of a planter in South Carolina, who, at his death, left her mother and his three children free, with money to go to St. Augustine, where they had relatives. It was during the Revolutionary War; and they were captured on their passage, carried back, and sold to different purchasers. Such was the story my grandmother used to tell me; but I do not remember all the particulars. She was a little girl when she was captured and sold to the keeper of a large hotel. I have often heard her tell how hard she fared during childhood. But as she grew older she evinced so much intelligence, and was so faithful, that her master and mistress could not help seeing it was for their interest to take care of such a valuable piece of property. She became an indispensable personage in the household, officiating in all capacities, from cook and wet nurse to seamstress. She was much praised for her cooking; and her nice crackers became so famous in the neighborhood that many people were desirous of obtaining them. In consequence of numerous requests of this kind, she asked permission of her mistress to bake crackers at night, after all the household work was done; and she obtained leave to do it, provided she would clothe herself and her children from the profits. Upon these terms, after working hard all day for her mistress, she began her midnight bakings, assisted by her two oldest children. The business proved profitable; and each year she laid by a little, which was saved for a fund to purchase her children. Her master died, and the property was divided among his heirs. The widow had her dower in the hotel which she continued to keep open. My grandmother remained in her service as a slave; but her children were divided among her master's children. . . .

To this good grandmother I was indebted for many comforts. My brother Willie and I often received portions of the crackers, cakes, and preserves, she made to sell; and after we ceased to be children we were indebted to her for many more important services. . . .

Little attention was paid to the slaves' meals in Dr. Flint's house. If they could catch a bit of food while it was going, well and good. I gave myself no trouble on that score, for on my various errands I passed my grandmother's house, where there was always something to spare for me. I was frequently threatened with punishment if I stopped there; and my grandmother, to avoid detaining me, often stood at the gate with something for my breakfast or dinner. I was indebted to her for all my comforts, spiritual or temporal. It was her labor that supplied my scanty wardrobe. I have a vivid recollection of the linsey-woolsey dress given me every winter by Mrs. Flint. How I hated it! It was one of the badges of slavery. . . .

When I had been working a month at the plantation, the great aunt of Mr. Flint came to make him a visit. This was the good old lady who paid fifty dollars for my grandmother, for the purpose of making her free, when she stood on the auction block. My grandmother loved this old lady, whom we all called Miss Fanny. She often came to take tea with us. On such occasions the table was spread with a snow-white cloth, and the china cups and silver spoons were taken from the old-fashioned buffet. There were hot muffins, tea rusks, and delicious sweetmeats. My grandmother kept two cows, and the fresh cream was Miss Fanny's delight. She invariably declared that it was the best in town. The old ladies had cosey times together. They would work and chat, and sometimes, while talking over old times, their spectacles would get dim with tears, and would have to be taken off and wiped. When Miss Fanny bade us good by, her bag was filled with grandmother's best cakes, and she was urged to come again soon.

There had been a time when Dr. Flint's wife came to take tea with us, and when her children were also sent to have a feast of "Aunt Marthy's" nice cooking. But after I became an object of her jealousy and spite, she was angry with grandmother for giving a shelter to me and my children. She would not even speak to her in the street. This wounded my grandmother's feelings, for she could not retain ill will against the woman whom she had nourished with her milk when a babe. The doctor's wife would gladly have prevented our intercourse with Miss Fanny if she could have done it, but fortunately she was not dependent on the bounty of the Flints. She had enough to be independent; and that is more than can ever be gained from charity, however lavish it may be. . . .

The next day my new mistress began her housekeeping. I was not exactly appointed maid of all work; but I was to do whatever I was told. Monday evening came. It was always a busy time. On that night the slaves received their weekly allowance of food. Three pounds of meat, a peck of corn, and perhaps a dozen herring were allowed to each man. Women received a pound and a half of meat, a peck of corn, and the same number of herring. Children over twelve years old had half the allowance of the women. The meat was cut and weighed by the foreman of the field hands, and piled on planks before the meat house. Then the second foreman went behind the building, and when the first foreman called out, "Who takes this piece of meat?" he answered by calling somebody's name. This method was resorted to as a means of preventing partiality in distributing the meat. The young mistress came out to see how things were done on her plantation, and she soon gave a specimen of her character. Among those in waiting for their allowance was a very old slave, who had faithfully served the Flint family through three generations. When he hobbled up to get his bit of meat, the mistress said he was too old to have any allowance; that when niggers were too old to work, they ought to be fed on grass. Poor old man! He suffered much before he found rest in the grave. . . .

A small shed had been added to my grandmother's house years ago. Some boards were laid across the joists at the top, and between these boards and the roof was a very small garret, never occupied by any thing but rats and mice. It was a pent roof, covered with nothing but shingles, according to the southern custom for such buildings. The garret was only nine feet long and seven wide. The highest part was three feet high, and sloped down abruptly to the loose board floor. There was no admission for either light or air. My uncle Phillip, who was a carpenter, had very skilfully made a concealed trap-door, which communicated with the storeroom. He had been doing this while I was waiting in the swamp. The storeroom opened upon a piazza. To this hole I was conveyed as soon as I entered the house. . . .

My food was passed up to me through the trap-door my uncle had contrived; and my grandmother, my uncle Phillip, and aunt Nancy would seize such opportunities as they could, to mount up there and chat with me at the opening. But of course this was not safe in the daytime. It must all be done in darkness.

DOCUMENT 4:

Diary of a Soldier from Illinois, 1862

Source: Charles Wright Mills, *Army Life of an Illinois Solider: Including a Day by Day Record of Sherman's March to the Sea* (Washington, DC: Globe Printing Co., 1906), 51.

Charles Wright Mills was born in Canton, Illinois, and volunteered for duty at President Abraham Lincoln's first call for soldiers. In 1861, he joined Company E in the Eighth Illinois Infantry and subsequently reenlisted. Mills survived the war and settled in Louisiana as a sugar planter until his death in 1883. He kept a diary of his service in the Union army, which his sister published posthumously along with his war letters. In the letter below he noted the late arrival of a holiday package. After a long day of foraging, the provisions from home were most welcome.

Bird's Point [Missouri], January 5, 1862

We received the box of provisions to-day in very good order considering the length of time they have been knocked about on the route. It came by freight by some mistake or other. The doughnuts were the only articles spoiled. They had moulded. I sent the box over from Cairo but was not here when it was opened, so that aside from one cake labeled from Aunt Nancy, I don't know where a thing comes from. I did recognize your home snaps, too, and thought there was something very familiar in the taste of a mince pie I ate, but I am too badly used up tonight to be sure of anything and tell you as I want to how very much we are obliged to our good mothers for their thoughtful care of us. I believe every boy in our mess received socks and mittens from home. . . . At 7 this morning I went over to Cairo with 50 men after forage for our teams. We stood around in the cold, mud and rain for five hours before we got to work and then the men had all run off but 15 or 18 and we had to roll bales of hay over a way almost impracticable —and all told it was a mean job and used me up nearly totally.

DOCUMENT 5:

Bread Riot in Richmond, 1863

Source: Library of Congress, Prints and
Photographs Division, reproduction
#LC-USZ62–42028.

*In an article titled "Altars of Sacrifice: Confederate
Women and the Narratives of War," historian Drew
Gilpin Faust claims that by 1863 "the emotional and
physical deprivation of Southern white women escalated."
These women had taken over the management of house-
holds and plantations in the absence of their husbands*

Document 5

and sons. *Sacrifice for the cause of preserving southern independence was revered during the early days of the conflict. Yet, as their hardships mounted, many wondered whether their efforts were being made in vain. Plantation organization crumbled as African Americans fled to the promise of freedom, and two years into the war many southern women lacked basic necessities like wood for fireplaces, adequate clothing for young children, and food for family members still at home. In Richmond, the very capital of the Confederacy, in April 1863 women who were infuriated at their government unleashed their anger by breaking into a government storehouse to take bread. On April 8, 1863, the* New York Times *quoted a Union captive who witnessed the outburst. He noted that the three thousand women involved were "armed with clubs, guns and stones" but were soon placated by Jefferson Davis, who promised them provisions. Events such as these must have been heartening for the Union since, as Faust argued, they indicated that "the Confederate ideology of sacrifice" was beginning to "lose its meaning and efficacy."*

DOCUMENT 6:

Lincoln Declares a Day of National Thanksgiving, 1863

Source: Library of Congress, *A Century of Lawmaking for a New Nation: U.S. Congressional Documents and Debates, 1774–1875,* Statutes at Large, 735–36.

The proclamation below initiated the precedent for the last Thursday of each November to be set aside as a day of national thanksgiving. Prior to Abraham Lincoln's declaration, some individual states celebrated a day of "thanksgiving" at different times. It was Sarah Josepha Hale, an influential magazine editor with a reader-

ship of forty thousand, who wrote a letter to the pres-
ident on September 28, 1863, advising him to have the
"day of our annual Thanksgiving made a National and
fixed Union Festival." She had been quite persistent, in
fact, having advocated for this national holiday for fif-
teen years. In this proclamation, originally drafted by
William Seward, Lincoln called upon a nation embroiled
in a war of "unequaled magnitude and severity" to offer
thanks to God and "fervently implore the interposition
of the Almighty Hand to heal the wounds of the nation."
The idea of a Thanksgiving dinner was emerging in some
places in the early nineteenth century and became more
common following this declaration. Yet, Lincoln's concep-
tion seemed to focus more on spiritual matters than on
physical sustenance.

By the President of the United States of America.
A Proclamation.
October 3, 1863

The year that is drawing towards its close, has been filled with the blessings of fruitful fields and healthful skies. To these bounties, which are so constantly enjoyed that we are prone to forget the source from which they come, others have been added, which are of so extraordinary a nature, that they cannot fail to penetrate and soften even the heart which is habitually insensible to the ever watchful providence of Almighty God.

In the midst of a civil war of unequaled magnitude and severity, which has sometimes seemed to foreign States to invite and to provoke their aggression, peace has been preserved with all nations, order has been maintained, the laws have been respected and obeyed, and harmony has prevailed everywhere except in the theatre of military conflict; while that theatre has been greatly contracted by the advancing armies and navies of the Union.

Needful diversions of wealth and of strength from the fields of peaceful industry to the national defence, have not arrested the plough, the shuttle or the ship; the axe has enlarged the borders of our settlements, and the mines, as well of iron and coal as of the precious metals, have yielded even more abundantly than heretofore. Population has steadily increased, notwithstanding the waste that has been made in the camp, the siege and the battle-field; and the country, rejoicing in the consciousness of augmented strength and vigor, is permitted to expect continuance of years with large increase of freedom.

No human counsel hath devised nor hath any mortal hand worked out these great things. They are the gracious gifts of the Most High God, who, while dealing with us in anger for our sins, hath nevertheless remembered mercy.

It has seemed to me fit and proper that they should be solemnly, reverently and gratefully acknowledged as with one heart and one voice by the whole American People. I do therefore invite my fellow citizens in every part of the United States, and also those who are at sea and those who are sojourning in foreign lands, to set apart and observe the last Thursday of November next, as a day of Thanksgiving and Praise to our beneficent Father who dwelleth in the Heavens. And I recommend to them that while offering up the ascriptions justly due to Him for such singular deliverances and blessings, they do also, with humble penitence for our national perverseness and disobedience, commend to His tender care all those who have become widows, orphans, mourners or sufferers in the lamentable civil strife in which we are unavoidably engaged, and fervently implore the interposition of the Almighty Hand to heal the wounds of the nation and to restore it as soon as may be consistent with the Divine purposes to the full enjoyment of peace, harmony, tranquillity and Union.

In testimony whereof, I have hereunto set my hand and caused the Seal of the United States to be affixed.

Done at the City of Washington, this Third day of October, in the year of our Lord one thousand eight hundred and sixty-three, and of the Independence of the United States the Eighty-eighth.

Abraham Lincoln
William H. Seward,
Secretary of State

DOCUMENT 7:

Union Officers Dining in the Field, 1864

Source: Library of Congress, Prints and
Photographs Division, reproduction #LC-
B8171–0132 DLC.

April of 1864 marked the end of the third full year of fighting during the Civil War. The Emancipation Proclamation had gone into effect that January, and many African Americans began the perilous journey to join the Union lines in search of freedom. Jefferson Davis declared that escaped slaves would be sent back to their owners. On

Document 7

the battlefront, General Ulysses Grant announced an offensive campaign in late April in which the Army of the Potomac was to attack the Army of Northern Virginia. The soldiers dining together in the image were photographed at Brandy Station, Virginia, which was the winter quarters for the Army of the Potomac in the winter of 1863–64. They may have very well been gearing up for Grant's spring offensive.

DOCUMENT 8:

Recipes and Counsel for Southern Women after the War, 1867

Source: Annabella P. Hill, *Mrs. Hill's Southern Practical Cookery and Receipt Book* (New York: Carleton Publisher, 1872).

Annabella P. Hill was born in 1810 and raised in Georgia. Her cookbook, Mrs. Hill's Southern Practical Cookery and Receipt Book, *which was first published in 1867, offered a wide range of culinary and housekeeping advice to wives who were facing the task of managing households in the wake of a devastating war, the loss of which was a tremendous blow to the South. Though she made only a couple of direct references to the recent conflict, the book was clearly positioned to help young women who were taking on the full duties of cooking and keeping house in the postwar era.*

Introduction

The book which meets the wants of the times deserves a place in every household, and the writer who, in these degenerate days, contributes to the pleasures, and at the same time advances the real welfare, of the race, deserves a place in the Calendar with all the benefactors of the age. "THE SOUTHERN PRACTICAL COOKERY AND RECEIPT BOOK" comes up to the standard here laid down. . . .

We are not just now in a condition to sacrifice much to fancy or ornament; we must address ourselves to the useful and substantial. Every mother, wife, and daughter must now become a practical operator in the domestic circle. Each should be emulous to excel in neatness, industry, usefulness and economy. The days for romance have passed, if they ever existed; the night for the dreamy visions of elegance and luxury in connection with a life of indolence has suddenly given place to the day of enterprise and industry. A crisis is upon us which demands the development of the will and energy of Southern character. Its prestige in the past gives earnest of a successful future. As woman has been queen in the parlor, so, if need be, she will be queen in the kitchen; as she has performed so gracefully the duties of mistress of the establishment in the past, so she will, with a lovelier grace, perform whatever labor duty demands. She has learned that the services of a good cook, that queen of the kitchen, are essential elements in the health, the good temper, the enjoyment and peace of every family; that the art of Cooking is the parent of all other arts, and eating and drinking the highest of all animal enjoyments. The race of good cooks among us is almost extinct. What shall be done to bring back the good old times, when a knowledge of the good housewifery demanded for the health and comfort of every family was not considered too low for the attention of any lady? Labor should not be held in disrepute by any, for it is written "In the sweat of thy brow shalt thou earn bread." . . .

Will not the ladies, whose opinions and actions form public sentiment, lead off in a culinary reform, which will correct the errors of the past, and introduce a system of industry and economy to meet the present emergencies? Reverse the present order of things. Make idleness and indolence disreputable, and labor and usefulness honorable. . . . I am most happy to be able to state that the reform here recommended has already begun, and is progressing most encouragingly. Our women have the will and intelligence; the practical development of the resources at their command is all that is necessary to insure success. The appearance of the "Southern Practical Cookery and Receipt Book" at this crisis augurs a new and brighter era in the culinary art.

Dedication

To young and inexperienced Southern housekeepers I desire to dedicate this work. In its preparation I have been influenced mainly by the consideration that in this peculiar crisis of our domestic as well as national affairs, counsel is needed—wise and timely counsel, which not only gives warning of dangers ahead, but, in language clear and unmistakable, teaches how they may be avoided. Thousands of young women are taking . . . themselves the responsibilities of housekeepers, a position for which their inexperience and ignorance of household affairs renders them wholly unfitted. Formerly "mother" or "mother's cook," or one whom the considerate mother had trained to fill this important office in the daughter's ménage, was, with many, the only authority considered necessary in the conduct of culinary operations. Now, however, things are changed. "Mother," even if within accessible distance, is too much occupied with the accumulated cares of her own establishment to be able to devote much time and attention to a separate one; while "mother's cook" and "trained servants" are remembered as among the good spirits that ministered to the luxury and ease of bygone days.

CHAPTER 6

Eating in an Age of Decadence and Empire

Rapid industrialization in the late nineteenth century created an expanding urban population, which was dramatically stratified along class lines. Businessmen like John D. Rockefeller, Andrew Carnegie, and Jay Gould amassed enormous fortunes as they produced the oil, steel, and railroads that fueled the economic expansion of the period. Decried as overreaching and unscrupulous, wealthy industrialists were often labeled "robber barons." Many members of this class indulged in conspicuous consumption that further tarnished their reputations. For example, Mamie Fish, the wife of Stuyvesant Fish, once hosted a dinner party in honor of her dog, who wore a $15,000 diamond collar to the event. The first document in this chapter, a 1903 cartoon from the satirical magazine *Puck*, ridicules the pretensions of wealthy diners.

An expanding urban middle class also indulged in elaborate dining rituals, using the table as a space to showcase their wealth and refinement. In document 2, Mary Foote Henderson gives entertaining advice designed to aid social climbers. The opulence of the era influenced aesthetic judgments about physical beauty, and women with curvaceous figures were admired. In document 5, T. D. Duncan offers advice on "how to be plump."

The luxuries enjoyed by the very wealthy and the financially comfortable were fueled by the labor of a vast working class. Between 1870 and 1920, more than 11 million Americans moved from rural areas to work in urban factories. They were soon joined by more than 25 million overseas immigrants who came to the United States between 1860 and 1920. These new arrivals brought new food habits with them, which eventually led to an expansion of the American palate.

Documents 7 and 8 explore contemporary responses to the introduction of Italian and Jewish foods.

At the same time that large numbers of immigrants were flocking to the United States, internal imperial ambitions led to the Spanish-American War in 1898. The conflict highlighted growing problems with the nation's industrial food supply as troops complained about being fed tainted and substandard fare. In document 10 Captain Frank E. Moore gives testimony about the inadequate provisioning of troops during the war.

DOCUMENT 1:

Criticism of Conspicuous Consumption, 1903

Source: Library of Congress, Prints and
Photographs Division, reproduction
#LC-DIG-ppmsca-25741.

This cartoon, which depicts ornately attired diners participating in a variety of themed dinners, offers a critique of the conspicuous consumption patterns of the rich during this period. The social elite of the era hosted elaborate dinner parties, serving multicourse feasts on tables laden with elegant crystal, silver, and china. A typical place setting contained ten pieces of flatware, with designated forks for oysters, fish, meat, salad, and fruit. Decorations and entertainment were equally elaborate. Expensive Turkish rugs were used to cover the lawn for an outdoor event in Newport, Rhode Island, in 1900, and a trained monkey was a guest of honor at another party in that city, a favorite summer playground for the wealthy.

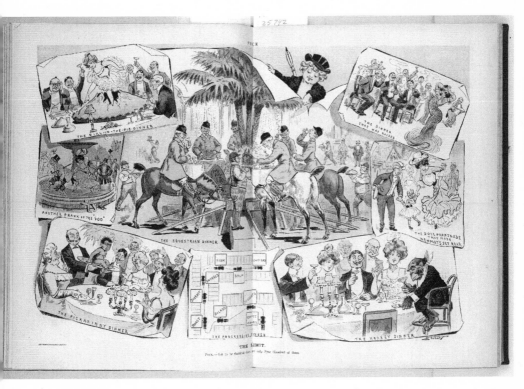

Document 1

DOCUMENT 2:
Dinner Party Etiquette in 1877

Source: Mary Foote Henderson, *Practical Cooking and Dinner Giving: A Treatise Containing Practical Instructions in Cooking; in the Combination and Serving of Dishes; and in the Fashionable Modes of Entertaining at Breakfast, Lunch, and Dinner* (New York: Harper & Brothers, 1877), 20–27.

The growing middle class of the late nineteenth century utilized dining practices as a way to demonstrate their prosperity and to separate themselves from members of the working class, whom they regarded as social inferiors.

Elaborate dining rituals, such as those described in
Practical Cooking and Dinner Giving *by Mary Foote*
Henderson, *were coordinated by middle-class women who*
were aided in these preparations by hired servants. Urban
middle-class women were no longer producers of food who
cultivated gardens, slaughtered animals, and made items
like cheese and beer at home. They had become consum-
ers who purchased food from the marketplace, including
an expanding array of industrially processed items, which
hired servants transformed into meals.

There are several hints about serving the table, which I will now spec-
ify separately, in order to give them the prominence they deserve.

1st. The waiters should be expeditious without seeming to be in a
hurry. A dragging dinner is most tiresome. In France, the dishes and
plates seem to be changed almost by magic. . . .

2d. Never overload a plate nor oversupply a table. It is a vulgar
hospitality. . . .

At a fashionable dinner party, if there are twelve or fourteen guests,
there should be twelve or fourteen birds, etc., served on the table—one
for each person. If uninvited persons should call, the servant could
mention at the door that madam has company at dinner. . . .

The French understand better than the people of any other nation
how to supply a table. "Their small family dinners are simply gems of
perfection. There is plenty for every person, yet every morsel is eaten.
The flowers or plants are fresh and odoriferous; the linen is a marvel
of whiteness; the dishes are few, but perfect of their kind. . . ."

3d. Never attempt a new dish with company—one that you are not
entirely sure of having cooked in the very best manner.

4th. Care must be taken about selecting a company for a dinner
party, for upon this depends the success of the entertainment. . . .

5th. Have the distribution of seats at table so managed, using some
tact in the arrangement, that there need be no confusion, when the
guests enter the dining-room, about their being seated. If the guest of
honor be a lady, place her at the right of the host; if a gentleman, at
the right of the hostess. . . .

6th. If the dinner is intended to be particularly fine, have bills of fare, one for each person, written on little sheets of paper smoothly cut in half, or on French bill-of-fare cards, which come for the purpose. . . .

Bills of fare are generally written in French. It is a pity that our own rich language is inadequate to the duties of a fashionable bill of fare, especially when, perhaps, all the guests do not understand the Gallic tongue, and the bill of fare (*menu*) for their accommodation might as well be written in Choctaw. . . .

If you are entertaining a ceremonious company, with tastes for the frivolities of the world, or, perhaps, foreign embassadors, use unhesitatingly the French bills of fare; but practical uncles and substantial persons of learning and wit, who, perhaps, do not appreciate the merits of languages which they do not understand, might consider you demented to place one of these effusions before them. I would advise the English bills of fare on these occasions.

7th. The attendants at table should make no noise. They should wear slippers or light boots. . . .

8th. The waiter should wear a dress-coat, white vest, black trousers, and white necktie; the waiting-maid, a neat black alpaca or a clean calico dress, with a white apron.

9th. Although I would advise these rules to be generally followed, yet it is as pleasant a change to see an individuality of a characteristic taste displayed in the setting of the table and the choice of dishes as in the appointments of our houses or in matters of toilet. . . .

10th. Aim to have a variety or change in dishes. . . .

11th. Although many fashionable dinners are of from three or four hours' duration, I think every minute over two hours is a "stately durance vile." . . .

12th. There is a variety of opinions as to who should be first served at table. Many of the *haut monde* insist that the hostess should be first attended to. . . . As soon as the second person is helped, there should be no further waiting before eating.

13th. Have chairs of equal height at table. . . .

14th. The selection of china for the table offers an elegant field in which to display one's taste. The most economical choice for durability is this: put your extra money in a handsome dessert set, all (except the plates) of which are displayed on the table all the time during dinner; then select the remainder of the service in plain white, or white and gilt, china. When any dish is broken, it can be easily matched and replaced. . . .

15th. I will close these suggestions by copying from an English book a practical drill exercise for serving at table. The dishes are served from the side-table.

"Let us suppose a table laid for eight persons, dressed in its best; as attendants, only two persons—a butler and a footman, or one of these, with a page or neat waiting-maid; and let us suppose some one stationed outside the door in the butler's pantry to do nothing but fetch up, or hand, or carry off dishes, one by one:

> While guests are being seated, person from outside brings up
> soup;
> Footman receives soup at door;
> Butler serves it out;
> Footman hands it;
> Both change plates.
> Footman takes out soup, and receives fish at door; while butler
> hands wine;
> Butler serves out fish;
> Footman hands it (plate in one hand, and sauce in the other);
> Both change plates.
> Footman brings in *entrée,* while butler hands wine;
> Butler hands *entrée*
> Footman hands vegetables;
> Both change plates,
> Etc., etc."

DOCUMENT 3:

The *Nation* Magazine Comments on the "Servant Problem"

Source: "Waiters and Waitresses," *Nation,*
December 10, 1874, 378–80.

During the late nineteenth century, middle- and upper-class families observed complicated dining rituals. At a dinner party, diners expected to be fed multicourse meals and to be seated at tables laden with china and flatware appropriate for each phase of the meal. These laborious standards of elegance were maintained through the efforts of domestic servants. Affluent housewives of the era despaired about finding servants who would skillfully and cheerfully perform the arduous tasks of housekeeping and publically lamented what became labeled the "servant problem." Because Irish immigrants frequently, if reluctantly, took these undesirable jobs, the incompetent servant was often personified as "Bridget" in the press. This article from the Nation *magazine makes suggestions about how to best train servants and advocates for the professionalization of female waitresses.*

We took the liberty pointing out two years ago that much of the prevalent complains against the deficiencies of Irish servant-girls was unreasonable, because it was based on an assumption which employers, while using it, well knew to be untenable. The rage poured out in most magazine articles over Bridget, for instance, draws an appearance of justifiability from the theory that Bridget offers her services as a trained servant, and is employed as such—the fact being that parties to the contract know perfectly well that this theory is without foundation. Bridget in reality offers her services as a person who knows little or nothing of the business expected of her, and who would not be engaged to do it if the other party to the contract could get it done in any other way. . . . In coming here they would find themselves in a position which even those who preach most against Bridget consider degrading, which every native American will almost sooner starve than fill, which both our politics and our literature do everything to depreciate, and from which nearly all Americans hold it to be the duty of either man or woman to escape at the earliest possible moment. No calling can flourish or attract capacity or elicit training under such conditions. The domestic servant in America, such as she is, is the natural product of the tone of the American community on certain important social questions, and the natural result of the depreciation visited on all forms of menial service. . . .

The training of waitresses is matter which can never be successfully undertaken until the prevailing notion that the Irish girls who offer themselves in that capacity are impostors—that is, persons who represent themselves as something which they are not has been abandoned, and until they are finally and fairly accepted as peasant girls, and nothing else. . . .

The fact is that when the Irish waitress first sees the dinner-table of a family of even moderate means and plain living, it bears to her somewhat the appearance of preparation for a mysterious heathen rite. The rule and regulations which control the setting of the table, the course of the dishes, the changing of the plates, and so on are provisions for the gratification of tastes she does not possess, and which only years of training would give her. . . . Explanation of the theory of the matter to her would therefore be impossible, for it is largely founded on faint repugnances and likings, which vanish as soon as we bring the cold eye of reason to bear on them. To try to make her feel about the table service as her mistress does—that is, give her the mistress's sense of propriety and decency and fitness—would be as absurd as to begin the education of a military recruit by a course of high strategy.

In all attempts to train persons in a very low stage of culture, and especially in attempts to train them to perform processes which they do not understand the theory, the only chance of success lies in making them repeat incessantly certain acts in an invariable order. By the incessant repetition you create a sort of habit, and by the invariableness of the order you help that feebleness of the memory for unfamiliar facts which almost always accompanied deficiency of mental training. Therefore, if anybody wants to train a peasant girl to wait at table, she must be made to do the same thing every in the same sequence, and with no omission departure from the programme. . . .

In order to enable one woman to wait efficiently on many guests, and enable a small establishment to have many guests, and to keep down noise, racket, and disorder, and give opportunity for conversation, the way to serve the dinner be it never so small or plain, is in courses—that is, to produce only one dish at a time, and give nobody any choice, and let anybody who does not like what is offered to him wait until something else comes. . . . The order of service can in this way be taught and learnt and remembered. This leads us to ask one question, in closing, of those who are interested in the industrial training of women, and that is, why there are in our large towns and cities, where dinner-giving is frequent, no extra-menial waitresses competent to take charge of a dinner as waiters do, to carve, and see to the proper service of a large company? There is in every city a considerable number of men who make a good living in this way. . . . Yet the number of women who have to follow waiting as a calling is very large everywhere; and there is a large number of others who say they would follow it if it were not that it confines them all day long in another person's house, and at her beck and call, and gives them no control over their own time. Now, there is not a single American city where waitresses who understood their business knew how to carve, and had the art of dressing neatly in black, might not obtain employment in large numbers at high wages November till April and yet live in their own lodgings. . . . Why is it that this had never been thought of by an elevator of women, or suffrage worker, or enlarger of woman's sphere, or thrower open of women to a greater variety of resources?

DOCUMENT 4:

Dinner at Delmonico's

Source: Library of Congress, Prints and Photographs Division, reproduction #LC-USZ62–139580.

This photograph of a 1906 dinner for the Sons of the Revolution in the State of New York at the famous Delmonico's restaurant captures the ambiance of the fine dining culture of the era. In 1828 Swiss immigrant John Delmonico and his brother Peter opened Delmonico & Brother, a pastry shop that served hot drinks and liqueurs. In 1831 they began serving hot food prepared by a French chef. Soon the restaurant boasted an elaborate eleven-page French menu and became an exclusive dining destination at a time when the United States had not yet developed an

Document 4

extensive public dining culture. In his American Notes,
*the novelist Charles Dickens reported being impressed
by the "unsurpassable, politeness, delicacy, sweet temper, [and] hospitality" he encountered at an 1868 dinner
hosted in his honor at Delmonico's. In keeping with the
opulence of the period, members of the New York City
elite who attended an 1873 "Swan Banquet" were served
from a table decorated to resemble a park, which included
a lake populated by live swans.*

DOCUMENT 5:

Advice on How to Achieve the Ideal Body Type in the Nineteenth Century

Source: T. D. Duncan, *How to Be Plump, Or
Talks on Physiological Feeding* (Chicago:
Duncan Brothers, 1878), iv–v, 20–24.

*In the late nineteenth century, a large body size was consid-
ered a sign of health and was deemed attractive. Women*

strove to have large busts and hips and tiny waists, which were artificially constricted by tightly laced corsets. While books on how to lose weight became increasingly popular after thinness became the height of fashion in the 1920s, prior to that some men and women strove to gain rather than to lose excess weight. How to Be Plump, *written by T. D. Duncan in 1878, advises its readers on what to eat to achieve the ideal standard of physical attractiveness of its day.*

PREFACE.

"How shall I get fleshy? I would give the world to be as plump as Miss ——!" "Poor child; it is nothing but skin and bone! I cannot bear to undress it! What shall I feed it that will fat it up?" "I would give a dollar a pound for more fat!" "I flesh up in winter, and then I feel so much better." "This climate agrees with me nicely; I never was so well and fleshy in my life." "Since I became fleshy I am very well, indeed." "She was thin and sickly, but now is the very picture of health." "When in Europe I was so fleshy, and had such an appetite!" "While drinking the water at —— I felt so much better and fleshed up." "The hot baths did me so much good; but cold baths make me sick." "I have fleshed up remarkably this year (a wet year), and feel, oh, so much better!" "When I weighed one hundred and forty pounds, I felt well; now I weigh only one hundred and ten pounds, and feel so miserable!" "What has fifteen or twenty pounds of fat to do with health?" Such are a few of the problems that cluster around. "How to cluster around HOW TO BE PLUMP," the solution of which this work attempts.

Why cannot "the picture of health" be painted in all faces? Why is plumpness associated with health, and leanness with disease? Why are "Americans proverbially lean?" These are vital questions that touch the philanthropic, interest the statesman, and arouse scientific investigation. The rules for healthy feeding are very simple, when once understood. The following pages have been prepared, to as to give them the widest dissemination with the hope that they may prove as valuable to every lean person, as their personal and professional application has been to

THE AUTHOR.

CHAPTER II.

Leanness a Disease,

You ask "is leanness a disease or a disease tendency?" That is a very practical question, as we shall see: The term *leanness* implies a simple absence of fat, and is not to be confounded with thinness and emaciation—terms expressing in different degrees the absence, not only of fat, but also of the gelatinous and albuminous tissues.

Leanness, when it cannot be referred to a satisfactory cause, must be accounted a disease. When extreme, it is usually accompanied by more or less thinness or emaciation—states of the system which if not explicable on obvious principles, must almost always be considered as morbid.

It is rare to see a person steadily gaining fat after any pathological reduction of weight, without a corresponding gain in amount and quality of blood.

Almost any grave change for the worse in health is at once betrayed in most people by a loss of fat, and this is readily seen in the altered forms of the face, which because it is the always visible, and in outline the most irregular part of the body, shows first and most plainly the loss and gain of tissue. . . .

The first thing which strikes an American in England, is the number of inordinately fat people, and especially fat women. This excess of flesh we usually associate in idea with slothfulness, but English women exercise more than ours, and live in a land where few days forbid it, so that probably such a tendency to obesity is due chiefly to climatic causes. To this also we may no doubt ascribe the habits of the English as to food. They are larger feeders than we.

The exciting causes of leanness may be considered under the heads of climate or locality; and diet and exercise. The inhabitants of mountainous and barren sandy regions are naturally disposed to be lean. Leanness, more than from any other cause, results from deficient or innutritious diet; from the free use of acid liquors, as cider, etc.; from excessive bodily and mental activity. . . .

Another cause of leanness is the lack of water. It is a strange fact that as a rule, lean persons drink little or no water. They say they do not crave it, therefore they do not drink it.

There is a restless anxiety about lean people that is distressing.

They look hungry, sad and irritable. As children they whine and cry and put all creation out of joint.

"The very thin must certainly, so to speak, live from hand to mouth, and have little for emergencies."

DOCUMENT 6:

Lillian Russell: A Nineteenth-Century Beauty

Source: Prints and Photographs Division, reproduction #LC-USZ62–77348.

Actress and singer Lillian Russell weighed two hundred pounds at the height of her fame and was considered a great beauty. By twenty-first-century standards, she would be considered obese. Russell was known for her appreciation of food and her robust appetite, and in a 1912 beauty advice column in the Spokane, Washington, Spokesman-Review *she advised, "Girls who wish to become plump must eat a variety of food."*

Document 6

DOCUMENT 7:

Italian Foodways Expand the American Palate

Source: Emma Paddock Telford, "Good Cookery," *Burlington Free Press*, September 24, 1903, 2.

Between 1880 and 1920, more than four million Italians immigrated to the United States, seeking better economic opportunities. Many had suffered from food deprivation at home and, ironically, could afford to eat more of the foods of their native regions after arriving in the United States. Immigrants from various parts of Italy developed a pan-ethnic cuisine, which was influenced by American taste sensibilities as well. For example, Italian American food tends to contain larger quantities of animal protein than the original cuisine. Mainstream American eaters were initially ambivalent about the food of these new-comers, and many found foods cooked with garlic and herbs too pungent. However, over time pasta and red sauce dishes made inroads into US public dining culture as well as into private kitchens. Recipes such as this one, published in Vermont in 1903, helped promote these foods. Their popularity peaked during World War I, when Americans became more curious about the foodways of their allies.

In an increasing number of American households macaroni, spaghetti and vermicelli, prepared in various ways, are becoming stock articles of the diet. This is an excellent thing from a dietic standpoint, as experiments have proved that flour in this form is more perfectly digested than even in bread.

Time was when the country received all its supply of the various macaronis from Italy, where the best macaroni in the world is made from the hard Italian flour. Excellent as is the Naples macaroni, the difficulty of drying it sufficiently to escape the attack of insects has lately lessened its importation to this country.

Nearly all the imported macaroni now comes from Lyons, France, but the constant improvement in the American product—of which Chicago alone offers 200 different varieties, will soon render any importation as unnecessary as "carrying coats to Newcastle."

That the Italians are past masters in the art of cooking macaroni cannot be denied: and the American housewife can do not better than to copy Italian methods. . . .

SPAGHETTI WITH BEEF (ITALIAN METHOD)

Put four even tablespoons of butter or olive oil in a large saucepan over the fire. When it bubbles, add two medium sized onions, sliced thin. Cover the pan, and cook until the onions are brown, put in the beef, well larded with strips of fat pork. As soon as the onions are brown, put in the beef and let it brown thoroughly, turning it over and on its sides until all are served. When this is accomplished add a can of tomatoes, of a superior brand or a dozen fine ripe tomatoes cut in quarters. Season with a few strips of parsley, a clove of garlic crushed, a bay leaf, a teaspoonful of kitchen bouquet, plenty of salt and a pinch of cayenne. Add a quarter of a cup of boiling water and in equal amount of white wine. Cover closely and simmer gently for two hours. Then add a pound of boiled ham, cut in dice, or smoked tongue if preferred. Pour in another grill of wine and a cup of hot water. Again cover and cook two or three hours longer—until perfectly tender and in "rags." Meanwhile cook a half pound of spaghetti in plenty of boiling salted water and drain. Now put the beef and seasonings into a colander and press every bit of juice through. Return to the saucepan and thicken with two tablespoonfuls of flour stirred to a paste in a little cold water. Put a layer of the spaghetti on a platter, sprinkle over it a layer of Parmesan, then a layer of the sauce. Next layer of spaghetti, more cheese, and sauce, until all the materials are used. Put a little olive oil or butter on top, brown in the oven and serve with a separate dish of the grated Parmesan.

DOCUMENT 8:

Jewish Immigrants Import Kosher Food Practices

Source: "Banquet of 'Kosher' Food," *New-York Tribune*, July 18, 1887, 10.

Between 1880 and 1924 more than two million Jewish immigrants from Eastern Europe dramatically expanded the Jewish population of the United States, particularly in New York City, where many migrants initially settled. Devout members of the community clung to kosher food practices, which restricted what kinds of foods could be eaten and how food had to be prepared. These rules were mystifying to outsiders who were unfamiliar with the religion. This 1887 article in the New-York Tribune *describes both the laws of kosher meals and the fare served at the proliferating number of Jewish-run restaurants in the city.*

[A kosher meal] differs from the ordinary dinner in many respects. Inasmuch as meats constitute the main feature of a heavy meal, and as nothing made from milk may be eaten at the same meal with meat, according to the Mosaic law, there can be no butter, cream nor cheese on the bill of fare. Shellfish are known as "unclean" in the Mosaic dietary laws. . . .

Kosher means simply "pure" or clean." . . .

Although strictly kosher restaurants are scattered thickly through the part of New-York known as the Ghetto, and although there are hundreds of butchers in the uptown districts who sell only kosher meat, there are only a few caterers in New-York who make a specialty of serving kosher dinners, but they do an extensive business. There are hundreds of Jewish households in the upper residence part of New-York where the old Mosaic dietary laws are strictly adhered to, and on festival occasions in those households the kosher caterer is called upon and furnishes dinners and suppers which compare favorably in quality with those of leading New-York establishments.

"Weddings are our strong point," said one of these caterers, with "bar-mitzvah parties a close second, and engagement festivals not far behind." The bar-mitzvah dinner is the function which takes place in the orthodox Jewish family on the day when a son, having attained his thirteenth birthday, is called before the altar in the synagogue, and there, in the presence of the congregation, declares his belief in the one ever-living God, and reads a passage from the Holy Writ, and by the ceremony becomes a responsible member of the community, while up to that time his parents had been responsible for him. . . .

WHAT IT TASTES LIKE

Many people who patronize the kosher restaurants say that there is nothing about the looks or taste of the various dishes served there to distinguish them from the articles served at the ordinary restaurants, but that is a popular error. The meats are all highly spiced and are invariably served with rich gravies. As neither butter nor cream may be used in preparing the vegetables they also often reach the table in a form which would make recognition by the American sense of taste impossible. The pastry is heavy in style, and gives the uninitiated cause for serious reflection. Still physicians whose practice is among those people who eat only kosher food say that they have fewer stomach troubles to fight than their brother practitioners whose patients would be afraid to eat kosher food.

DOCUMENT 9:
Food Vendors in New York City

Source: Library of Congress, Prints and Photographs Division, reproduction #LC-USZC4–1584.

In the early twentieth century the Lower East Side of New York City was the most densely populated neighborhood in the world. It was home to many recent immigrants. Many made their living selling familiar foreign foods to other new arrivals. For example, Jewish vendors sold bagels and knishes, which have since become iconic New

Document 9

York foods. In this photograph, neighborhood residents congregate on the street buying and selling fresh produce.

DOCUMENT 10:

Source: *Report of the Commission Appointed by the President to Investigate the Conduct of the War Department in the War with Spain* (Washington, DC: Government Printing Office, 1900).

Captain Frank N. Moore Testifies about the Quality of Military Food Supplies during the Spanish American War

General Major Miles A. Davis created the "Embalmed Beef Scandal" when he claimed in 1898 that tainted meat had been served to US troops serving in Puerto Rico and Cuba during the Spanish-American War. Among others, Theodore Roosevelt provided testimony claiming that the meat rations smelled like chemicals and caused illness to those who consumed them. However, an official investigation into these allegations concluded that the meat was of a low quality but not unsafe. In this passage, Captain Frank N. Moore responds to questions posed by military officials about the quality of military food supplies during the conflict.

Q. [Will you tell me about the state of the] commissary supplies?

A. Yes, sir. I do not think at any time in that camp we had enough water to give the men what they needed. I would make the statement that to the best of my knowledge there never was a day when the men had a sufficient supply of water. Many a day we received only one or one and a half barrels of water.

Q. What was the character of your commissary supplies in general?

A. Good.

Q. Did the men have sufficient in quantity for their wants?

A. Yes, sir; of the kind that they got.

Q. What was it as to quality?

A. Generally good.

Q. Were there any exceptions; if so, what?

A. The principal exception was on potatoes. I think that from 40 to 50 percent of the potatoes issued to us were rotten.

Q. Did you return the potatoes?

A. Never in but one instance. I ordered the quartermaster to return the potatoes, and he did so and was placed under arrest.

Q. To whom did you return them?

A. To the regimental quartermaster.

Q. You didn't do that again, then?

A. No, sir; I had orders from both the colonel and the regimental quartermaster that we were to take all of the food that was issued to us; what we couldn't use we were to bury.

Q. Did you ever have a board of survey to condemn any of your food?

A. No, sir.

Q. And in accordance with the directions of the colonel of your regiment and of your regimental quartermaster, did you bury any of your food and if so, how much?

A. We buried it for some time, until we did not have ground sufficient to dig and bury it, and then we burned all that we could. We burned the meat and potatoes.

Q. Did you get bad meat at any time?

A. Frequently.

Q. What meat?

A. The pork and bacon.

Q. What was the trouble with it?

A. Maggots.

Q. All the way through? Did you cut into it?

A. No, sir. When we found pieces with maggots on the outside we simply threw it on the fire.

Q. You didn't know then that the commissary at the depot would have issued you meat in place of what was bad and would have given you good potatoes in place of what were bad if they had been taken to the depot?

A. No, sir; our orders were to take what we got. . . .

I went to the quartermaster and protested against sending us any more rotten potatoes, and he notified me we were to take the supplies to be issued and what we couldn't use we were to bury or burn. I went to the colonel and got the same orders. The other troubles we had on the food question was with green coffee and our beef spoiling on us.

Q. What did you do in that case when the beef spoiled?

A. Burned it.

Q. And got nothing in return?

A. No. Don't understand that the meat was spoiled when we got it. The meat was issued at 9 o'clock in the evening, and we would proceed to cook it either right off or after breakfast. The meat was usually in fair condition, but was spoiled the next day.

Q. It was meat taken out of a refrigerating car?

A. Yes, sir.

Q. It wouldn't spoil after it was cooked?

A. Yes, sir; it would spoil as quickly after it was cooked as before. By skinning off the outside we could usually use some for dinner; but very, very rarely.

Q. That meat ought to be issued in the morning?

A. They found it more practicable. I don't wish to be understood to say that the beef was bad when issued to us. The pork was; but the beef would spoil within ten or twelve hours. We tried to manufacture a refrigerator. We had one made with such lumber as we could get, but were unable to get the ice.

DOCUMENT 11:

Taft Banquet Highlights US Imperial Interests

Source: Library of Congress Prints and Photographs Division, reproduction #LC-USZ62–53396.

Before he became the twenty-seventh president of the United States in 1908, William Howard Taft served as

Document 11

the governor-general of the Philippines, then a US colony. This lavish banquet decorated with a tropical theme can be seen as a metaphor of imperialism as the guests at the table consume a representation of a foreign country.

CHAPTER 7

Food and Social Reform in the Progressive Era

The rapid industrialization of the US economy in the late nineteenth and early twentieth centuries created widespread social change. Technological innovations gave consumers access to an unprecedented variety of foods. Networks of railroads and canals facilitated the rapid transportation of perishable items over vast distances and, in combination with the proliferating supply of canned goods, these developments meant that Americans no longer had to depend solely on seasonally and locally produced food. However, some industrially produced food was adulterated or otherwise unsafe. Document 2 is an excerpt from Upton Sinclair's 1906 novel, *The Jungle*, which documents unsanitary conditions in meat-processing facilities. Anxiety over modern life and changes in the food supply led some to follow the precepts of reformers like John Harvey Kellogg, who advocated an unprocessed, vegetarian diet and taught that foods such animal products, condiments, and spices contributed to unhealthy sexual desires.

For many Americans, however, just having enough to eat was a primary concern. The working people whose labor provided the backbone of the industrial economy suffered as a result of poor pay and crowded and dismal urban living conditions. Immigrants faced the additional struggle of acclimating to a foreign culture. Middle-class reformers of the era used a variety of tactics to attempt to remedy the difficulties of urban life. Many became convinced that food habits were an important avenue of social reform and that proper eating habits could ameliorate poverty, cure alcoholism, and end crime. In document 5, Pearl Idelia Ellis argues that Mexican Americans should change their traditional food habits as a means of assimilation and self-improvement. Document 6 is a photograph of Native American students at the Carlisle Indian Industrial School who were given instruction in European American styles of cooking under the same rationale.

The linkage of food habits and ideas about virtue prepared middle-class Americans to restrict voluntarily their consumption during World War I, when the federal government engaged in a propaganda campaign designed to convince Americans to conserve food to aid in the war effort. The government poster depicted in document 10 urges US citizens to preserve food and, in the process of conservation, to "Can the Kaiser."

DOCUMENT 1:

John Harvey Kellogg Gives Dietary Advice to Adolescent Girls

Source: J. H. Kellogg, *Ladies Guide in Health and Disease* (Des Moines, IA: Condit and Nelson, 1866), 176–77.

In the 1830s, minister, dietary reformer, and temperance advocate Sylvester Graham became well known for advocating a vegetarian diet that consisted primarily of whole grains and vegetables. He believed that meat and spicy foods were "stimulating" and encouraged sexual desires and masturbation, which he deemed harmful. His ideas were enormously influential. Although most Americans did not give up meat, whole wheat "Graham" flour began to appear in many nineteenth-century recipes. One of the greatest advocates of his ideas was John Harvey Kellogg, a medical doctor who became director of the Battle Creek Sanitarium health facility. Along with his brother, Will Keith Kellogg, he invented corn flakes, which he originally served as a health food to his patients but which ultimately became one of America's most popular breakfast foods. In this passage from an 1866 handbook about women's health, Kellogg advocates a bland, largely vege-

tarian diet for adolescent girls. In large part, this diet was intended to curb sexual appetites.

Hygiene of Puberty . . .

The most strict attention should be given to every habit of life which relates to mental and physical health. The interests of the girl's moral nature should also receive attention, as the turbulent condition of both mind and nervous system which frequently occurs at this period of the girl's existence, needs the calming and soothing effects of wholesome religious influences.

Great care should be taken that a sufficient amount of wholesome and nutritious food is eaten regularly and at proper hours. At this period, the appetite is often capricious, and frequently new and strange appetites are developed which need to be restrained, while there may be suddenly manifested a strange aversion for the simple and wholesome food which has before been eaten with relish. Fruits and grains should chiefly constitute the diet. Oatmeal, cracked wheat, graham bread, milk, and fruit, with various grain preparations, furnish the very materials which are most needed for the proper development of the system at this time, and in the very best possible form. Meat should be used sparingly. The idea that girls at this time require a large amount of mutton, beef-steak, eggs, and other stimulating and exciting food, is a very great mistake. It is much better that the system should be undisturbed by stimulating influences of any sort.

DOCUMENT 2:
Upton Sinclair Publicizes Unsanitary Conditions in Meat-Processing Facilities

Source: Upton Sinclair, *The Jungle* (1906).

In 1904 the novelist Upton Sinclair took a job in a meat-packing plant in Chicago in order to conduct research for a novel about the poor working conditions endured by unskilled immigrant laborers. In spite of his intentions, what really captured the public's attention after the 1906 appearance of his novel, The Jungle, was his description of the unsanitary environment inside the meat-packing facility. Sinclair despairingly remarked, "I aimed at the public's heart, and by accident I hit it in its stomach." His vivid descriptions of animal processing helped fuel the pure food movement and led to the passage of the 1906 Pure Food and Drug Act, which made it illegal to adulterate or mislabel foods shipped across state lines.

Hog Slaughtering

It was a long, narrow room, with a gallery along it for visitors. At the head there was a great iron wheel, about twenty feet in circumference, with rings here and there along its edge. Upon both sides of this wheel there was a narrow space, into which came the hogs at the end of their journey; in the midst of them stood a great burly Negro, bare-armed and bare-chested. He was resting for the moment, for the wheel had stopped while men were cleaning up. In a minute or two, however, it began slowly to revolve, and then the men upon each side of it sprang to work. They had chains which they fastened about the leg of the nearest hog, and the other end of the chain they hooked into one of the rings upon the wheel. So, as the wheel turned, a hog was suddenly jerked off his feet and borne aloft . . . [and] one by one they hooked up the hogs, and one by one with a swift stroke they slit their throats. There was a long line of hogs, with squeals and lifeblood ebbing away together; until at last each started again, and vanished with a splash into a huge vat of boiling water.

It was all so very businesslike that one watched it fascinated. It was porkmaking by machinery, porkmaking by applied mathematics. And yet somehow the most matter-of-fact person could not help thinking of the hogs; they were so innocent, they came so very trustingly; and they were so very human in their protests—and so perfectly within their rights! They had done nothing to deserve it; and it was adding insult to injury, as the thing was done here, swinging them up in this cold-blooded, impersonal way, without a pretense of apology, without the homage of a tear. . . .

One could not stand and watch very long without becoming philosophical, without beginning to deal in symbols and similes, and to hear the hog squeal of the universe. Was it permitted to believe that there was nowhere upon the earth, or above the earth, a heaven for hogs, where they were requited for all this suffering? Each one of these hogs was a separate creature. Some were white hogs, some were black; some were brown, some were spotted; some were old, some young; some were long and lean, some were monstrous. And each of them had an individuality of his own, a will of his own, a hope and a heart's desire; each was full of self-confidence, of self-importance, and a sense of dignity. And trusting and strong in faith he had gone about his business, the while a black shadow hung over him and a horrid Fate waited in his pathway. Now suddenly it had swooped upon him, and had seized him by the leg. Relentless, remorseless, it was; all his protests, his screams, were nothing to it—it did its cruel will with him, as if his wishes, his feelings, had simply no existence at all; it cut his throat and watched him gasp out his life. And now was one to believe that there was nowhere a god of hogs, to whom this hog personality was precious, to whom these hog squeals and agonies had a meaning? Who would take this hog into his arms and comfort him, reward him for his work well done, and show him the meaning of his sacrifice?

Sausage Making

There was never the least attention paid to what was cut up for sausage; there would come all the way back from Europe old sausage that had been rejected, and that was moldy and white—it would be dosed with borax and glycerine, and dumped into the hoppers, and made over again for home consumption. There would be meat that had tumbled out on the floor, in the dirt and sawdust, where the workers had tramped and spit uncounted billions of consumption germs. There would be meat stored in great piles in rooms; and the water from leaky roofs would drip over it, and thousands of rats would race about on it. It was too dark in these storage places to see well, but a man could run his hand over these piles of meat and sweep off handfuls of the dried dung of rats. These rats were nuisances, and the packers would put poisoned bread out for them; they would die, and then rats, bread, and meat would go into the hoppers together. This is no fairy story and no joke; the meat would be shoveled into carts, and the man who did the shoveling would not trouble to lift out a rat even when he saw one—there were things that went into the sausage in comparison with which a poisoned rat was a tidbit. There was no place for the men to wash their hands before they ate their dinner, and so they made a practice of washing them in the water that was to be ladled into the sausage. There were the butt-ends of smoked meat, and the scraps of corned beef, and all the odds and ends of the waste of the plants, that would be dumped into old barrels in the cellar and left there. Under the system of rigid economy which the packers enforced, there were some jobs that it only paid to do once in a long time, and among these was the cleaning out of the waste barrels. Every spring they did it; and in the barrels would be dirt and rust and old nails and stale water—and cartload after cartload of it would be taken up and dumped into the hoppers with fresh meat, and sent out to the public's breakfast. Some of it they would make into "smoked" sausage—but as the smoking took time, and was therefore expensive, they would call upon their chemistry department, and preserve it with borax and color it with gelatine to make it brown. All of their sausage came out of the same bowl, but when they came to wrap it they would stamp some of it "special," and for this they would charge two cents more a pound.

DOCUMENT 3:

A Multiethnic Dinner Party in the Age of Immigration

Source: Library of Congress, Prints and Photographs Division, reproduction #LC-DIG-ppmsca-28430.

This 1883 illustration from the popular magazine Puck *depicts a dinner party with Uncle Sam and his "adopted children." Designed as a commentary on how the rapid influx of immigrants during the late nineteenth century was creating an increasingly multiethnic society, the drawing also captures some of the racial attitudes of the day.*

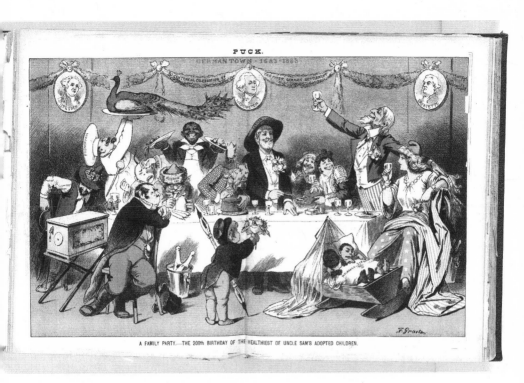

A FAMILY PARTY.—THE 200th BIRTHDAY OF THE HEALTHIEST OF UNCLE SAM'S ADOPTED CHILDREN.

Document 3

DOCUMENT 4:

Catherine E. Beecher and Harriet Beecher Stowe Advocate for the Training of Housewives

Source: Catherine E. Beecher and Harriett Beecher Stowe, *Principles of Domestic Science; As Applied to the Duties and Pleasures of Home* (New York: J. B. Ford and Company, 1870), 13, 17–18, 148.

Beginning in the mid-nineteenth century, a growing number of women advocated for the professional training of housewives, arguing that the domestic tasks that were considered "women's work" were not accorded the same respect as work performed by men outside of the home in part because women did not receive proper vocational training. Increasingly, women such as Catherine Beecher and Harriett Beecher Stowe referred to housekeeping as "domestic science" to emphasize the technical difficulty of cooking and cleaning. The apex of this movement came when Ellen Richards, author of The Chemistry of Cooking and Cleaning, *was offered a position as a faculty member of the Massachusetts Institute of Technology in 1884.*

The authors of this volume, while they sympathize with every honest effort to relieve the disabilities and sufferings of their sex, are confident that the chief cause of these evils is the fact that the honor and duties of the family state are not duly appreciated, that women are not trained for these duties as men are trained for their trades and professions, and that, as the consequence, family labor is poorly done, poorly paid, and regarded as menial and disgraceful.

To be the nurse of young children, a cook, or a housemaid, is regarded as the lowest and last resort of poverty, and one which no woman of culture and position can assume without loss of caste and respectability.

It is the aim of this volume to elevate both the honor and the remuneration of all the employments that sustain the many difficult and sacred duties of the family state, and thus to render each department of woman's true profession as much desired and respected as are the most honored professions of men. . . .

This can be secured only by a true view of the grea[t] end designed by the family state which Jesus Christ came into this world to secure. What, then, is that end?

It is to provide for the training of our race to the highest possible intelligence, virtue, and happiness, by means of the self-sacrificing labors of the wise and good, and this with chief reference to a future immortal existence.

The distinctive feature of the family is self-sacrificing labor of the stronger and wiser members to raise the weaker and more ignorant to equal advantages. The father undergoes toil and self-denial to provide a home, and then the mother becomes a self-sacrificing laborer to train its inmates. . . .

XIII. GOOD COOKING.

There are but a few things on which health and happiness depend more than on the manner in which food is cooked. You may make houses enchantingly beautiful, hang them with pictures, have them clean and airy and convenient; but if the stomach is fed with sour bread and burnt meats, it will raise such rebellions that the eyes will see no beauty anywhere. The abundance of splendid material we have in America is in great contrast with the style of cooking most prevalent in our country. How often, in journeys, do we sit down to tables loaded with material, originally of the very best kind, which has been so spoiled in the treatment that there is really nothing to eat! Green biscuits with acrid spots of alkali; sour yeast-bread; meat slowly simmered in fat till it seemed like grease itself, and slowly congealing in cold grease; and above all, that unpardonable enormity, strong butter! How one longs to show people what might have been done with the raw material out of which all these monstrosities were concocted!

There is no country where an ample, well-furnished table is more easily spread, and for that reason, perhaps, none where the bounties of Providence are more generally neglected. Considering that our resources are greater than those of any other civilized people, our results are comparatively poorer.

It is said that a list of the summer vegetables which are exhibited on New York hotel-tables being shown to a French *artiste* he declared that to serve such a dinner properly would take till midnight. A traveler can not but be struck with our national plenteousness, on returning from a Continental tour, and going directly from the ship to a New York hotel, in the bounteous season of autumn. For months habituated to neat little bits of chop or poultry, garnished with the inevitable cauliflower or potato, which seemed to be the sole possibility after the reign of green-peas was over; to sit down all at once to such a carnival! to such ripe, juicy tomatoes, raw or cooked; cucumbers in brittle slices; rich, yellow sweet-potatoes; broad lima-beans, and beans of other and various names; tempting ears of Indian-corn steaming in enormous piles; great smoking tureens of the savory succotash, an Indian gift to the table for which civilization need not blush; sliced egg-plant in delicate fritters; and marrow-squashes, of creamy pulp and sweetness; a rich variety, embarrassing to the appetite, and perplexing to the choice.

Verily, the thought must often occur that the vegetarian doctrine preached in America leaves a man quite as much as he has capacity to eat or enjoy, and that in the midst of such tantalizing abundance he has really lost the apology, which elsewhere bears him out in preying upon his less gifted and accomplished animal neighbors.

But with all this, the American table, taken as a whole, is inferior to that of England or France. It presents a fine abundance of material, carelessly and poorly treated. The management of food is nowhere in the world, perhaps, more slovenly and wasteful. Every thing betokens that want of care that waits on abundance; there are great capabilities and poor execution. A tourist through England can seldom fail, at the quietest country-inn, of finding himself served with the essentials of English table-comfort—his mutton-chop done to a turn, his steaming little private apparatus for concocting his own tea, his choice pot of marmalade or slice of cold ham, and his delicate rolls and creamy butter, all served with care and neatness. In France, one never asks in vain for delicious *cafe-au-lait*, good bread and butter, a nice omelet, or some savory little portion of meat with a French name. But to a tourist taking like chance in American country-fare, what is the prospect? What is the coffee? what the tea? and the meat? and above all, the butter?

DOCUMENT 5:

Pearl Idelia Ellis Argues that Dietary Reform Can Aid in Assimilation and End Crime

Source: Pearl Idelia Ellis, *Americanization through Homemaking* (Los Angeles: Wetzel Publishing Co., 1929), preface, 19, 26, 30–31.

Many domestic scientists believed that training house-keepers could not only improve the quality of family life but also solve a variety of social problems. Some dietary reformers worked with immigrants and ethnic minorities, urging them to abandon their food traditions in favor of what they deemed proper "American" cuisine, a bland diet heavily influenced by English food habits. They advocated for these changes not only as a means of assimilation but also as a way to cure societal ills ranging from crime to alcoholism. In this excerpt from her 1929 book Americanization through Homemaking, *Pearl Idelia Ellis focuses on trying to change the diet of Mexican American students in the public school system.*

If we assimilate the countless number of Mexicans that cross our southern border, either legally or otherwise, to better their condition in a new land, we must begin at the basic structure of their social order—the home.

The efforts of the Neighborhood Houses and charitable organizations furnish relief for the time being and deal with adults, who for the most part are unchangeable. Our main hope lies in the rising generation, and the public school is the greatest factor in its development.

Since the girls are the potential mothers and homemakers, they will control, in a large measure, the destinies of their further families. The teacher of homemaking has a large field for instruction. Hers is not a mere calling but an opportunity. It is she who sounds the clarion call in the campaign for better homes. . . .

If we expect them to adopt our customs, our ideals, and our country, let us set them a most worthy example. . . .

FOODS

Mexican families are mal-nourished, not so much from a lack of food as from not having the right varieties of foods containing constituents favorable to growth and development.

It is not expected that the average Mexican girl in our elementary school can comprehend chemical terms as applied to Household Science, but we can teach her a general knowledge of foods for regulating, building, and furnishing energy to the body, also the methods of preparing, cooking, and serving them.

Here again, a system of budgeting is necessary. How much shall they spend for food? How large a variety of proper foodstuffs can she purchase with the amount of money at her disposal? How can she furnish a diet necessary for the child, for the aged, and for the working man? All this involves a careful system of marketing. . . .

THE SCHOOL LUNCH

The noon lunch of the Mexican child quite often consists of a folded tortilla with no filling. There is no milk or fruit to whet the appetite. Such a lunch is not conducive to learning. The child becomes lazy. His hunger unappeased, he watches for an opportunity to take food from the lunch boxes of more fortunate children. Thus the initial step in a life of thieving is taken. . . .

NUTRITION AND CRIME

Nutrition plays a very important part in our lives, and affects us for good or ill. The old adage, "As a man thinketh, so is he," might easily be translated to, "As a man eateth, so is he," for his thinking is controlled to a greater extent than we are wont to realize by his eating and digestive processes. Efficient brain power is not found in an undernourished people. Nowhere is this better illustrated than in a Mexican community in a year when the supply of cheap labor exceeds the demand. Men congregate in idle groups. The severe strain falls on the housewife who deals out sustenance to each member of her family from her meager and disappearing supply of foodstuffs. The crisis comes. The pangs of hunger are accelerators of criminal tendencies. Forgery and stealing follows. The head of the family lands in jail. The rest of the family are helpless, and soon become county charges. Property owners pay taxes for their maintenance.

If we can teach the girls food values and a careful system of budgeting; how to plan in prosperity for the day of no income and adversity, we shall avoid much of the trouble mentioned here, in the future. Children will not come to school then without breakfast.

Employers maintain that the man with a home and family is more dependable and less revolutionary in his tendencies. Thus the influence of the home extends to labor problems and to many other problems in the social regime. The homekeeper creates the atmosphere, whether it be one of harmony and cooperation or of dissatisfaction and revolt. It is to be remembered that the dispositions, once angelic, become very much marred with incorrect diet and resultant digestive disturbances. . . .

DOCUMENT 6:
A Cooking Class at the Carlisle Indian Industrial School, 1901

Source: Francis Benjamin Johnston, *Carlisle Indian School Cooking Class*, 1901, Library of Congress, Prints and Photographs Division, reproduction #LC USZ62–26783.

The Carlisle Indian Industrial School, which operated from 1879 to 1918, was a model for a number of other Indian boarding schools established around the same time. The goal of these institutions was to assimilate Native American children into mainstream culture.

Document 6

Students were forced to assume English names, to attend Christian churches, to speak the English language, and to wear school uniforms. Female students received domestic training designed to prepare them to work as servants in white homes as well as to encourage them to disrupt traditional Native American food practices as a means of assimilation.

DOCUMENT 7:

Mary Hinman Abel Creates Recipes for the Economically Disadvantaged

Source: Mary Hinman Abel, *Practical Sanitary and Economic Cooking Adopted to Persons of Small or Moderate Means* (Rochester, NY: E. R. Andrews, 1889), 143–51.

Although the late nineteenth century was a time of opulent, multicourse dinner parties for the wealthy, many Americans struggled just to have enough food to eat. Forty percent of the working class lived below the poverty line of $500 a year. Many domestic scientists hoped to aid the impoverished, not by advocating for increased wages and a less lop-sided distribution of wealth, but by giving advice on how to stretch meager food resources. Mary Hinman Abel's award-winning 1889 Practical Sanitary and Economic Cooking Adopted to Persons of Small or Moderate Means *gives sample menus and advice to the economically disadvantaged. Her book also yields insights into contemporary medical knowledge about proper nutrition. Although scientists knew that foods could be classified as carbohydrates, fats, or proteins, they did not yet know that vitamins were vital for good health. Thus Abel felt free to advise the poor to save money by skimping on green vegetables.*

INTRODUCTION TO BILLS OF FARE, CLASS I.
(To the Mother of the Family.)

... We have learned that to keep us in good health and working order we ought to have a certain amount of what is best furnished by meat, eggs, milk and other animal products, and that we must also have fats as well as what is given us in grains and vegetables.

But now our work has only just begun for we are to furnish these food principles in the shape of cooked dishes to be put on the family table three times a day, and the dishes must not only be nourishing but they must taste good, and there must be plenty of variety from day to day; and last—and this is the hardest point of all—we are to try to do this for the sum of *13 cents per person daily.*

I am going to consider myself as talking to the mother of a family who has six mouths to feed, and no more money than this to do it with. Perhaps this woman has never kept accurate accounts and does not know whether she spends more or less than this sum. She very likely has her "flush" days and her "poor" days according to the varying amounts of the family earnings, and it may be a comfort to her to know that if she could average these days and plan a little better, she can feed her family nicely on this sum.

A few facts as to what the writer knows to have been done in this line will not be amiss. I knew a family of 6 belonging to one of the professional classes, half, grown people, and half, children, that lived for a year on an average of 11 cents per person daily, and no one would have said that they did not live well enough; they had meat about four days out of the seven, there was always cake on their supper table, and they used plenty of fruit.

Here is an average bill of fare. Breakfast—milk toast, fried potatoes, coffee; dinner—soup made of shank of beef, fried liver, rice and potatoes; supper—bread and butter fried mush, stewed pears and cake. Next day there was pressed beef made from the soup meat chopped and flavored, and the next day there was cheap fish nicely fried. The head of this household was a skillful economist, absolutely no mistakes were made in cooking, and not a scrap was wasted, she had a long list of simple dishes at her command and she especially studied variety. ...

It must be mentioned that the price on which this family lived in comfort could not have been as low as it was but for one great help; they had a small garden that furnished green vegetables and a little fruit. But then almost every family has some special advantage that would lower the rate somewhat; one buys butter or fruit advantageously of friends in the country, another can buy at wholesale when certain staples are cheapest, still another may be able to keep a few fowls, and so on. . . .

Another thing, when I speak of a woman who is to buy the food of a family for 13 cents apiece daily, I have in mind the wife of a man who earns this sum himself, the wife having her time to attend to the housework and children. If a woman helps earn, as in a factory, doing most of her housework after she comes home at night, she must certainly have more money than in the first case in order to accomplish the same result, for she must buy her bread already baked and can only cook those dishes that take the least time. . . .

I only ask you in advance to try the recipes I shall give and to try to lay aside your prejudices against dishes to which you are not accustomed, as soups and cheese dishes for instance. You cannot afford to reject anything that will vary your diet, for many good tasting things you cannot buy. . . .

In buying meat your saving cannot be so much in quantity as in quality. Try to learn the different parts of an animal, and to distinguish between meat from a fat ox and that from a lean one, for, as we have explained, the former has less water in it, and why should you pay good money for that which nature gives you free? In winter, try to buy meat ahead so that you can make it tender by keeping it, and you will notice, too, that the larger the piece you buy the smaller is the per cent of bone you get with it. . . . As we have said again and again in these pages, the low-priced or tougher parts have as much nutriment for you as the rib roast which is beyond your purse. . . .

In buying eggs, you must be governed by the price; in winter use as few as possible, and even in the spring when they are cheapest, remember that they are not as cheap as the lowest priced cuts of meat from fat animals. But when they cost only 15 cents a dozen you can well disregard any small comparison of nutritive values, in consideration of their high worth in furnishing variety; you can afford to use them now and then in the place of meat and in making the various egg dishes.

Of the value of cheese as a regular dish to take the place of meat, you can read in another part of this essay. Buy it once a week at least, the skim variety, if you cannot afford the others, and grate or cook it according to the recipes given.

Try to find a reliable milkman and buy skim milk at half the price of full, and use it for all cooking purposes, keeping full milk, and, if possible, a little of the cream, for coffee.

Now let us take the vegetable part of your diet. You must keep on hand every kind of flour and grain that is not too expensive; be thankful that wheat flour is so good and so cheap, it will be your best friend. . . .

Except in the height of their season, have nothing to do with green vegetables, at least not under the impression that they are cheap; if you buy them, know that you are paying for flavors and variety, rather than for food. But even in the early spring, buy plenty of such vegetables as onions, carrots, parsley and other green herbs for your soups and stews. When you go for a walk in the country, be sure to bring home mint and sorrel in your pocket; the former will make you a nice meat sauce, the latter a delightful flavor in soup. It will be perfectly easy for you to grow in a window box that delicious herb, parsley, and have it always fresh.

For a low purse, there is no help so great as a knowledge of flavorings. When we remember that we can live on bread, beans, peas and a little cheap meat and fat the year round if we can only make it "go down," we shall realize the importance of such additions as rouse the appetite; there is room here for all your skill and all your invention. . . .

BILLS OF FARE, CLASS I.

For family of six, average price 78 cents per day, or 13 cents per person.

SATURDAY, MAY.

Breakfast.
Flour Pancakes, with Sugar Syrup.
Coffee.

Dinner.
Bread Soup.
Beefneck Stew.
Noodles.
Swelled Rice Pudding.

Supper.
Browned Flour Soup, with Fried Bread.
Toast and Cheese.

DOCUMENT 8: A

New York City Tenement Kitchen Doubles as a Home Workshop in 1911

Source: Library of Congress Prints and
Photographs Division, reproduction
#LC-DIG-nclc-04111.

This photograph captures the cramped living conditions of the urban working class in the early twentieth century. The woman, identified as Mrs. Palontona, and her daughter Michaeline are making lace in the kitchen of their tiny apartment.

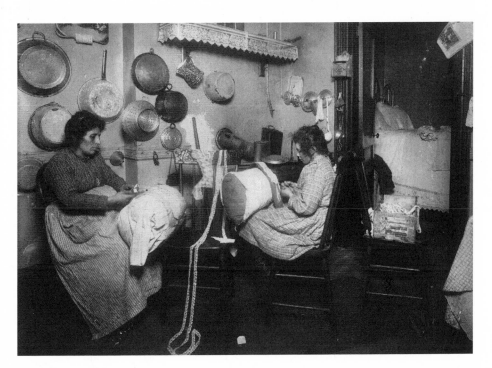

Document 8

DOCUMENT 9:

The US Food Administration Asks for Voluntary Food Conservation during World War I

Source: Food Administration, *Food Administration Bulletins* (Washington, DC, 1919).

Herbert Hoover, the director of the US Food Administration during World War I, asked Americans to conserve food voluntarily during the conflict to help feed the troops and allies. Among other things, the government asked Americans to conserve wheat and to substitute other grains such as corn in their daily diets and to consume less meat, particularly red meat. In general, middle-class

Americans were more likely to adhere to government suggestions than working-class Americans who were more concerned about finding enough food to feed their families than with following elaborate schemes of food substitution. The federal government created an expansive propaganda campaign to try to increase participation.

Do You Know Corn Meal?

ITS USE MEANS Service to Your Country

Nourishing Food for You

Try corn bread and see how good it can be. There are many kinds. You will wonder why you didn't use it every day before the war. It is very nourishing, too. A cup of corn meal gives even more fuel to your body than a cup of wheat flour. Here is a quick kind of corn bread. Our grandmothers used to bake it on a board before the open fire. You can bake it in your oven.

Corn Dodger

2 cups corn meal.

1 teaspoon salt.

2 teaspoons fat.

1¾ cups boiling water.

Pour the boiling water over the other materials. Beat well. When cool, form into thin cakes and bake 30 minutes in a hot oven. Makes 14 biscuits. These crisp little biscuits are good with butter or gravy. Eat them with your meat and vegetables.

STUDY THESE FIVE FOOD GROUPS

Every food you eat may be put into one of these groups. Each group serves a special purpose in nourishing your body. You should choose some food from each group daily.

1. VEGETABLES AND FRUITS.

2. MILK, EGGS, FISH, MEAT, CHEESE, BEANS, PEAS, PEANUTS.

3. CEREALS—CORN MEAL, OATMEAL, RICE, BREAD, ETC.

4. SUGAR, SIRUPS, JELLY, HONEY, ETC.

5. FATS—BUTTER, MARGARINE, COTTONSEED OIL, OLIVE OIL, DRIPPINGS, SUET.

You can exchange one food for another in the same group.

For example, oatmeal may be used instead of wheat, and eggs, or sometimes beans, instead of meat; but oatmeal can not be used instead of milk. Use both oatmeal and milk.

YOU NEED SOME FOOD FROM EACH GROUP EVERY DAY —DONT SKIP ANY

INSTEAD OF MEAT

CHEESE.

MILK.

EGGS.

BEANS.

PEAS.

CEREALS.

NUTS.

THESE make appetizing dishes to take the place of meat, Why not use them oftener? There are plenty of good ways of cooking them. They give you a body-building material, the protein, and they give a lot of it. The child to grow must have food that furnishes this kind of material. You need it, too. Even if you are grown up, you must have it to renew parts of your body used up by work and exercise. Don't think you have to eat meat to get this protein. These other foods have it, too. Take cottage cheese, for example. It is richer in this material than meat. You can eat a third of a cup of it with pleasure, and this third of a cup will give you as much of the protein as a quarter of a pound of sirloin steak—a good, generous serving. Or if you like baked beans, eat a cupful to give you the same amount of protein.

Use Less Meat—Our Government Needs It.

DOCUMENT 10:

The Federal Government Equates Food Behavior with Military Behavior during World War I

Source: Library of Congress Prints and Photographs Division, reproduction #LC-USZ62–76848.

During World War I, the federal government asked Americans to alter voluntarily their eating habits by conserving certain items in order to support the war effort. Patriotic citizens who agreed to follow the federal program could proudly display a Food Administration decal on a window of their homes. Women and children, in particular, were targeted by a propaganda campaign, which often equated food conservation with military engagement. Children could imagine themselves as combatants by joining the "School Garden Army." This poster encourages home canning not only as a means of feeding families on the home front but also as a way to "can" the Kaiser as well.

Document 10

CHAPTER 8

From Prohibition to the Great Depression

After World War I came to a close in 1919, the newly elected president, Warren G. Harding, promised a "return to normalcy" when he entered office in 1921. Pro-business Republicans occupied the White House for the next decade and Progressive Era reforms were traded for a more laissez-faire approach to the economy. Consumerism grew significantly in the 1920s as new appliances like radios and refrigerators were becoming available. The image of a "roaring" decade of frivolous partying may have been true for some, especially the wealthy who lived in big cities. However, farmers were suffering from a sluggish economy, and African Americans left the South in droves seeking alternatives to sharecropping or tenant farming. The Eighteenth Amendment banned the manufacture, sale, and transportation of alcohol in 1919, prompting some to lament by singing the "Prohibition Blues," a song that appears here as document 2. The illegal distribution of alcohol also encouraged the growth of organized crime, leading the government to reverse its position with the Twenty-First Amendment in 1933.

The stock market crash in 1929 ushered in an unprecedented economic crisis. The documents in this chapter capture the uncertainty many Americans faced when trying to feed themselves during these lean years. Frustration with Herbert Hoover's perceived lack of action to restore the economy led Franklin Delano Roosevelt to win the 1932 presidential election in a landslide. Roosevelt's sweeping New Deal policies focused on immediate recovery and future security. The Agricultural Adjustment Act, which was ultimately ruled to be unconstitutional, attempted to curb overproduction and to raise the prices on staple crops. The law, however, had the unintended consequence of leaving many tenant farmers out of work and without homes.

Displaced farmers impacted by the drought of the Dust Bowl took to the road in the hope of finding migrant work on farms in California. Document 6 is a photograph of a transient family sharing a meal on the roadside. New Deal job creation programs like the Tennessee Valley Authority and the Rural Electrification Agency helped provide electricity to rural areas. These families could now take advantage of new electrical appliances for the first time. Contemporary improvements in kitchen technology are depicted in document 8. Despite FDR's massive legislative overhaul, many families still could not make ends meet and lived a haphazard existence working odd jobs, waiting in lines for bread or soup, and sending children to school where they might be fed lunch. Document 9 reveals that some families depended on the generosity of local grocers who helped keep families alive during those years of scarcity.

DOCUMENT 1:

Migration and Memories of Food

Source: Chalmers S. Murray, "Fish, Hominy and Cotton," Library of Congress, American Life Histories: Manuscripts from the Federal Writers' Project, 1936–1940, 1–20 (excerpts).

July Geddes was an African American farmer and day laborer who was born and raised on Edisto Island, South Carolina. Work was sometimes in short supply, so he traveled outside of his home state to large cities, hoping to find work. Hundreds of thousands of African Americans made similar journeys during and following World War I. So many African Americans moved from their native South to places like Chicago and New York that the phenomenon became known as the Great Migration. Ethnic neighborhoods like Chicago's South Side and Harlem in New York developed as the numbers of southern African American migrants swelled. Foods from home, like greens and fried chicken, were now commonly prepared and sold in other regions of the country. Unlike many African Americans who left the region permanently, July Geddes had such a fondness for the tastes of the South, especially the fresh seafood and produce, that he decided to return.

July went to school for four years. Then he quit to help his father on the farm. The old man was getting stiff in his joints and thought that too much book learning was foolishness. A boy of eleven was old enough to handle a shovel and guide a mule down the furrows, for a few hours at least. He was also old enough to go into the woods and cut down small trees and load the high wheel cart with compost to scatter on the cotton field. July was a tough little fellow and didn't mind hard work so much. He ran away and played when the chance offered and took his beating with a resigned air. Life wasn't half bad when you could steal off once in awhile and "go crik."

Those days in the creek when the sun shone hot and the sea breezes dried the perspiration on your face; with line overboard and nothing to do but to wait until a fish nibbled; a watermelon under the bow seat and maybe some sweet bread for lunch; the jerk on the line that transmitted vibrations to your fingers, and then the fight to land the fish; the line cutting the water like a razor blade, the fish floundering around in the bottom of the boat while you are trying to take the hook out of its mouth; later when it was so hot that you couldn't stand it a minute longer, jumping overboard stark naked, dark copper flesh gleaming in the sun, your form swallowed by the blue-green water; trudging home with the fish strung on a blade of marsh grass, walking two miles through the burning sand, the trees casting no shadows because it was noon, then sitting on the door steps eating fried bass and rice for dinner—these early creek days are what July likes best to remember. . . .

For awhile things went well with July. He planted every available acre in sea island cotton, and worked it with loving care. Little attention was paid to corn or vegetables. Long staple cotton represented real money. You could always buy corn and oats for the horse and the cow could eat grass and wild herbs. Chickens could be raised on scraps and what they picked up, and hogs on slops. He thought that it would always be this way—borrowing from the factor in January, planting cotton in April, harvesting the crop in the fall, paying the factor in December and in January starting all over again. . . . In 1918 the boll-weevil came and sea island cotton died. . . . In 1924 he became disgusted with conditions and left for New York City.

July had never earned as much money in his life. It was almost unbelievable. He had landed a job as a stevedore down at the Marine docks and for every hour he worked he drew ninety-six cents. He lived close and began sending money home. He knew little of New York but Harlem and the docks on East River. Once he thought that he would explore Broadway and he started out bravely at the Battery and walked as far as Tenth Street. But the . . . crowds and the blare of automobile horns and the policemen frightened him and he dodged into a side street. He never walked on Broadway again.

He liked New York well enough but he said that he was homesick for . . . family and the farm, and the creek filled with good free food. . . .

July is now sixty-one, but still sturdy and able to do a full day's work behind the plow on in the ditch. . . . He continues to plant cotton. Now it is the short staple variety that he once so thoroughly despised. He has increased his corn and peas acreage, and he even cultivates a vegetable garden for he says that it would be a living shame to throw away the seed that the government gives him. July keeps a few hogs and one cow, and with the proceeds of the WPA wages that he drew for several years, he has almost finished paying for a mule. . . .

The Geddes have never heard of a balanced diet. They buy what their appetites call for—if they have the money. If the money is lacking they make out with the second or third choice. It is as simple as that. One can live a long time on sweet potatoes . . . grits, coffee sweetened with molasses, and fish or oysters.

"Hominy is the need battle of the house," says July. "Can't do without hominy for breakfast, eat um for dinner too if we ain't got rice. Vegetable kind—yes we place vegetable 'pon the table if the pig or the weather ain't destroy the garden. Mary is uh good canner. She put up plenty of peach, okra, tomato and so forth last year, for God send uh good season. Ain't see much fruit except what Mary jar and what the chillun send we from New York."

"Rice, now—we never get we fill of rice. Always cook um for dinner when we got um in the house. Mary cook uh quart and uh half one meal. Go splendid with oyster stew. . . ."

The head of the house is a cook in his own right. "I can cook uh pot of stew that will make you bite your tongue," says July with pride in his voice. "I take some butts meat and slice um thin and brown um over and let um boil long with uh mess of shrimp and okra and tomatoes. When it done you going to overeat yourself if you don't watch out."

July generally arises at six, winter mornings, unless it is Sunday, when he sleeps a little later. He thrown water over his face and then goes out and feeds the mule and the chickens. If there are any potatoes on hand he given a few to the cow. Around seven he eats a hearty breakfast, consisting of hominy, corn bread, butts and coffee. He goes to the field immediately after breakfast and remains there until the noon day meal is put on the table. An hour later he in back in the field. He knocks off at four o'clock. This allows him time to feed the animals and bring in wood before sunset. If there are no visitors or no church meeting to attend, he goes to bed soon after supper.

July longs for lay-by time in August. Then he can put the plow in the shed, lay the hoe aside and take a two week's vacation. Most of the holiday will be spent in the creek. It will be hot then. Watermelons will be ripe and channel bass hungry for shrimp.

DOCUMENT 2:

Bemoaning the Approach of Prohibition, 1917

Source: Historic American Sheet Music Collection, Rare Book, Manuscript, and Special Collections Library, Duke University.

The campaign to prohibit alcohol had roots in the nineteenth century and gained steam during the Progressive Era. Groups like the Women's Christian Temperance Union and the Anti-Saloon League lobbied for the prohibition of alcohol on both religious and practical grounds.

Chief among the concerns of women was the neglect and abuse of mothers and children by alcoholic fathers. Certain immigrant groups, like Germans, were viewed as poor workers because they spent so much time in beer halls or taverns. Some employers hoped that Prohibition might generate a more stable and reliable workforce. It was the circumstances of the First World War that ultimately led to the passage of the Eighteenth Amendment. Grain, it was thought, should be saved to produce food rather than alcoholic beverages. Also, German Americans were major producers of beer, and supporting their products while at war against the Germans seemed unpatriotic. Not everyone, however, was pleased about Prohibition. Popular songs—such as "Prohibition Blues" by Al Sweet (1917)— humorously grieved the censure of beloved refreshments.

"Prohibition Blues"

Mose Brown came a staggerin' home one morn,
Tears in his eyes and lookin' all forlorn,
His wifey met him with such an awful frown,
Said he "My dear, now won't you please sit down
and listen to me while a sad tale I relate,
of de news I hear what got me in dis state,
Last night I went to church and I feel so blue,
What that parson say I will tell to you:"

Oh! my Brothers and Sisters, listen to what I say
By nineteen twenty dere'll be no boose sold in the U.S.A.
De whole country am goin' bone dry,
Prohibition am de battle cry,
'Scuse me while I shed a tear,
For good old whiskey, gin and beer.
Goodbye forever, Goodbye forever
Ah got de Prohibition, Prohibition, Prohibition blues.

I got up and walked right out of dat church,
On the steps then I met old Sam'l Birch,
"Why Moses," he say, "what make you look so blue?"
I tell him an' he say
"If dat am true, Dat dry times comin'
An' dere goin' to can de booze,
come on to the corner, dere's no time to lose."
So we just started in drinkin' gainst dat day,
When I'd try to stop, then old Sam would say:

Oh! my Brothers and Sisters, listen to what I say
By nineteen twenty dere'll be no boose sold in the U.S.A.
De whole country am goin' bone dry,
Prohibition am de battle cry,
'Scuse me while I shed a tear,
For good old whiskey, gin and beer.
Goodbye forever, Goodbye forever
Ah got de Prohibition, Prohibition, Prohibition blues.

DOCUMENT 3:

Raid on Alcohol, early 1920s

Source: Library of Congress, Prints and
Photographs Division, reproduction
#LC-USZ62–123257.

Once the Eighteenth Amendment became law, police cracked down on the illegal sale of alcohol. Scenes like the one below in which authorities destroyed alcohol became more common. In this image, New York City deputy police commissioner John A. Leach made sure that the contraband was disposed of properly.

Document 3

DOCUMENT 4:

Anti-Saloon League Program, 1937

Source: Twenty-Ninth National Convention
of the Anti-Saloon League of America, An
American Time Capsule: Three Centuries
of Broadsides and Other Printed Ephemera,
Library of Congress, Rare Book and Special
Collections Division.

*Even after the Eighteenth Amendment was repealed, the
Anti-Saloon League remained active and still hoped to
rally prohibition sentiment once again. The statement
below appeared on an Anti-Saloon League convention
program from 1937, when the group criticized the increased
use of alcohol, especially by women.*

The Problem of the Convention

Liquor conditions now are worse than ever before. The 107,851 old saloons have been replaced by 419,587 new, modern, efficient sales agencies for intoxicating beverages. Millions of women and girls now are regular drinkers in thousands of places shrewdly designed to capture their patronage. Cocktail lounges, hotel bars, beer parlours, dance hall bars, liquor stores, groceries, soda fountains, filling stations, road houses, restaurants, old saloons, and new saloons almost everywhere now sell beverage alcohol.

Neon lighted signs along the streets, forests of billboards along the highways, acres of advertising in the newspapers and magazines, continual radio reminders on the air, all inviting everyone to drink, drink, drink!

Over 253 million gallons of distilled spirits, mostly whiskey, were produced in 1936—more than double the largest annual pre-prohibition production. The consumption of beer, wine and spirits increased 62 per cent during the past year over the first full year of legalized sale. These figures do not include the business of the bootleggers still numerous but less noticeable in the general downpour of drink.

At least 1,350,000 girls and women are now employed in our America to sell beer, wine and whiskey to men. A major crime is committed somewhere in the nation every 20 seconds. In 1936 automobile accidents resulted in an all time record of 37,708 killed and many thousands crippled, in spite of a nation wide frenzy of safety campaigns. The number of children killed in traffic, from 5 to 14 years of age, increased 10 per cent in 1936.

Overshadowing all in the picture of wet America is the realization that the liquor evil now is only getting started. What will conditions be when today's customs and habits have grown and ripened to the harvest? There is enough anti-liquor sentiment in this country to change the present situation. It must be mobilized through information and organization into aggressive action against the alcohol evil.

DOCUMENT 5:

Difficulty Finding Tenants

Source: J. Thompson, "Tenant Trouble," Library of
Congress, American Life Histories: Manuscripts
from the Federal Writers' Project, 1936–1940.

*The Agricultural Adjustment Act of 1933 helped to raise
crop prices as well as the income of farmers by regulating
the supply of food staples like corn, wheat, rice, tobacco,
and milk. However, the benefits were felt primarily by
landowners. Tenant farmers and sharecroppers, who
worked land owned by other farmers, still often lived a
precarious existence. Sharecroppers rarely got out of the
debt they owed landowners, and tenant farmers struggled
to feed their families on meager incomes. To further com-
plicate matters, tenant farmers, who were often very poor,
had the reputation of being indolent whether or not that
characterization was deserved. The narrative below was
told from the point of view of a farmer in North Carolina
who is frustrated that he cannot find an agreeable tenant.*

"After I married, I took up dairying. My wife's oldest sister was married
to a dairyman. You can see his place next door." He pointed to the
white farmhouse beside the tree-shaded stream near the highway, and
to [its] concrete barns and outbuildings. "Two of her brothers was in
the dairy business. They all live in this neighborhood. Naturally, I tried
dairying. I've stuck to it right steady ever since, except the two years I
tried running the corn mill."

"The biggest trouble a landowner has," Bill declares, "is getting
men on his place who are willing to work. Last year I had a . . . farm
just out of town, and I put a man by the name of Andrews to run
it for me. I got Ben off the county. He's about 50 years old, and he's
able-bodied. He has a wife and seven children. At that time they was
all on relief. His wife was workin' in a sewing room, and they got commodities off the county."

"Ben's a good farmer," continued Bill, "and he started out well. He put in some good crops: corn, beans, peas, potatoes, cabbage, cucumbers, and tomatoes, and he had a patch of tobacco. When I put in a cannery for my wife, I put [one] in for Mrs. Andrews, too."

Georgia, Bill's wife, took up the story: "I canned our surplus vegetables with the help of Ben's daughter Clara.

Bill paid Clara for helping me, and she lived with us. She's a nice, capable girl, just the age of my daughter, but while Hazel, who is 16 years old, is graduating this year from high school as valedictorian, Clara's family has moved about so much that she's just in the fifth grade. I wanted to keep her with us and send her to school with our children, but you never know how such people will turn out.

"I made an average of $1 a day on the vegetables I canned and sold to the school cafeteria," declared Georgia, "but Ben and his wife let their vegetables rot, quantities of them in their garden."

"About the middle of the summer" said Bill, "I found Ben was usin' my team to peddle whiskey. That's the last thing I'd stand for, so I told Ben the bootlegging would have to stop."

"After that, Ben lost interest in the farm," added Georgia, "and Bill has to get a lawyer after him to get the potatoes out of the ground."

"Yes, and he let [acres] of the corn burn up in the field; and the tobacco began disappearing out of the patch," interrupted Bill. "Ben was sellin' it and keepin' all the money. I [chased] around to all the tobacco warehouses, but I never found any of the tobacco. Next thing I [knew] that rascal was sellin' bootleg again. I could'a had him arrested, of course, but I felt sorry for his wife and children."

"Bill discharged him then," said Georgia.

"What became of him?" I asked.

"He was arrested for bootlegging, and they bound him over to the . . . court. He's out on bond."

"And his family?" I queried.

"Heaven knows!" said Georgia. "Back on relief, I reckon."

"Did you ever get a satisfactory tenant?"

"I didn't try," Bill replied. "I couldn't afford to lose any more money fooling with tenants. Ben cost me enough. I didn't rent it this year. It'll be cheaper for me to buy whatever feed I have to have. Mr. Reynolds couldn't get a good sharecropper, either, and nobody wanted to rent the place for cash, so he got disgusted, tore down the house, and put the land in grass."

DOCUMENT 6:

Family Praying over Meal by Roadside, 1939

Source: Library of Congress, Prints and
Photographs Division, reproduction
#LC-USF33–012275-M5 DLC.

*The Farm Securities Administration (FSA) was a New
Deal program created in 1937 and, like its predecessor,
the Resettlement Administration, was charged with aiding farmers who were struggling because of the Great
Depression and the Dust Bowl. Under the leadership of
Roy Stryker, the FSA employed a cadre of photographers
who faithfully documented the effects of the economic crisis. Many of the iconic images of the Depression era, which
have since become world famous, were taken by FSA photographers like Dorothea Lange and Gordon Parks. The
image below of a migrant family sitting down to eat by
the side of a road in Oklahoma was taken by Russell Lee.
Many itinerant families lived in abject poverty with all of*

Document 6

their belongings piled onto an old truck or crowded in a temporary shanty. This multigenerational family takes the time to pray before their noonday meal.

DOCUMENT 7:

Children Return to School Hoping for Free Lunch, 1939

Source: Carl T. Garrison, "Begging Reduced to a System," Library of Congress, American Life Histories: Manuscripts from the Federal Writer's Project, 1936–1940.

In the narrative below, a mother struggled to feed her children and hoped that the local school could at least provide them a nutritious lunch. Like many would-be breadwinners, her husband had difficulty finding long-term employment. The Works Progress Administration (WPA) was a massive New Deal agency that created jobs through a variety of public works programs such as erecting transportation infrastructure and public buildings. However, these projects were sometimes temporary or seasonal. As the men drifted from job to job, they often left behind families who struggled to obtain enough daily food.

BEGGING REDUCED TO A SYSTEM

Four Garrett children, the oldest a girl of fifteen, huddled at the door of the principal's office in the public school. When asked why they had been absent from school for five weeks, the children could give no intelligible answer. The idea uppermost in their minds was that their mother had told them to ask for free lunches. They were scantily clad for a November day. Their clothes were clean, but they seemed to have on little underclothing and . . . neither coats nor sweaters. Their shoes were full of holes. The group was obviously under-nourished, thin, pasty of complexion, anemic. One of the teachers . . . said, "They look just like poor little rats."

The principal reached for the telephone. He called the State Aid worker assigned to the school. "Mrs. Holt, look up the Garrett children; you know the address," he said. "Find out why they have been absent from school for five weeks, and why they wish to be put on the free lunch list. They are always asking for something."

A few minutes later the worker parked her car near a large, yellow house on a sparsely settled street inhabited mostly by negroes. After a few minutes, Mrs. Garrett came out and stood with her visitor on the windy porch. She was a thin woman, about thirty-three years old, with a pasty complexion, and projecting teeth. Her hair was much too yellow—drug store gold. Although the morning was raw and cold she wore a thin, sleeveless summer dress and no wrap.

"Yes, I live here," she said, hugging herself to keep warm; "me and my husband and our six children live in three rooms, upstairs."

The Henson's, who are her parents, and their youngest daughter and orphaned grandchildren occupy the lower floor.

She explained the children's absences. No, they had had measles long ago; it was the children under school age who had it now. "My husband had been out of work for nine weeks," she declared. "When we was asked to leave the cabin whar we wuz livin;" pointing to a tiny, log house in a hollow across the street, "we tuk the children and went to my brother's at Emma looking for work." That was five weeks ago.

"No'm, we didn't find no work. But my husband and me tuk in washin'. He'd go out and get the clothes, and help me do them. Then he got back on WPA and we come back to Asheville." She explained that her husband had been on the WPA for some time. The project on which he was working "run out," as she put it. So he had been suspended until work could be found for him elsewhere.

"He has always been a hard worker," she maintained. He had worked in the mills. He had been a clerk in a grocery store at $12 a week. He had been a truck driver for the city, and for various transfer companies. Before the depression, he had made $20 a week.

"We lived real well there," she said. "But there wasn't as many of us."

But for the past few years he had worked mainly as an unskilled laborer on the WPA.

"He goes back to work tomorrow," she said. "After he gets his first pay check, we can get along. But we haven't had anything in the house to eat for a week now but two messes of flour and a peck of meal. The children has nothin' for breakfast but a biscuit or a slice of corn bread. They come home after school begging for food. But I can't give them but two meals a day. That's why I want to get free lunches."

So the family was given commodities by the welfare department; beans, flour, and dried milk. The school agreed to give them lunches, and a member of the parent-teacher association offered to find clothes and shoes for them.

DOCUMENT 8:

Rural Electrification Agency Improves Kitchens, 1930s–1940s

Source: Library of Congress, Prints and Photographs Division, reproduction #LC-USW4-019827.

Document 8

The Rural Electrification Agency was a New Deal program funded through a corporate tax that brought electricity to rural homes. Around 80 percent of farms still lacked electricity in the early 1930s. Congress reasoned that introducing electricity into these homes would enable families to purchase new appliances, which would improve their kitchens while boosting the consumer economy. The agency was quite successful in that, by 1950, 90 percent of US farms had access to electricity, and many rural families had purchased electric stoves and refrigerators, like those in the image above. Kitchens like the one above facilitated faster cooking times and were safer since there was no need to build fires.

DOCUMENT 9:

Ethnic Grocery Store in Houston

Source: Photograph courtesy of Frank E. Tritico Jr.

Francesco L. Tritico, on the left in the photo below, immigrated to the United States from the village of Poggioreale, Sicily, in the late nineteenth century. Though many Italians and Sicilians entered the United States through New York, a large number of Sicilians, like Francesco, headed south instead and entered through ports on the Gulf of Mexico like New Orleans. Francesco labored in the sugarcane fields until he earned enough money to move to Texas. By the early twentieth century, he had sent for his wife, Mary Cangelosi Tritico, who is pictured below on the right, and they settled in a community where other Sicilians lived. Harrisburg had been important during the struggle for Texas independence and was a vital railroad junction until the late nineteenth century. By the time the Triticos opened their grocery store on Harrisburg Avenue, the

Document 9

neighborhood was on its way to being incorporated into Houston. The Triticos were well known in the community because of their store, which they operated through the Great Depression. It was the economic crisis of the 1930s, however, that ultimately caused the grocery to close. Francesco often extended credit to hungry families who needed essentials even when he knew there was little chance that they could settle their debt. Historian Hasia Diner's study of immigrant communities, Hungering for America, *points out that food was central to Italian cultural identity. Grocery stores like the Triticos' "wound the fabric of the community around food." This family knew hunger from their homeland and were not going to let their neighbors want for food as long as they had the means to help them. Francesco's great-grandchildren recall that even as late as the 1980s and 1990s, strangers in Houston would sometimes ask if they were related to the Triticos who ran the store on Harrisburg Avenue. These strangers would offer their thanks because the Triticos' grocery had helped keep their families alive during the Depression.*

CHAPTER 9

Wartime Food and Postwar Consumption

The grip of the economic depression began to loosen as the United States mobilized for war in the early 1940s. President Franklin Roosevelt introduced the idea of the "Four Freedoms"—freedom of speech, freedom of worship, freedom from want, freedom from fear—to Americans in 1941, and these became the foundation of the case for war. Defining freedoms to which every citizen could relate clearly positioned the Allies as representatives of democracy and in direct contrast with the Fascist enemy. As document 1 in this chapter demonstrates, freedom from want was often illustrated with food and reminded Americans that the scarcity they might be experiencing was far less acute than the deprivation and starvation of occupied nations.

Though rationing had been voluntary during the World War I, it was mandatory during World War II. Rationing applied to essentials like gasoline, but its major focus was on food items. As a main provider for the Allies, the US government explained that much of the food the country produced had to be diverted to the war effort. A point system was devised that set limits on the amount of goods like sugar and canned fruits and vegetables that a household could purchase. Women shoppers had to be resourceful as they learned the system and decided how to best balance the needs of their families with what foods were available. Document 2, a consumer information guide produced by the federal government, describes the conservation program. Inspired by patriotism and a desire to support the war effort, many women planted "victory gardens" or learned how to bake with less sugar.

The war also facilitated cultural exchange across continents. American GI's traveled to England and France, where they encountered new foods. Likewise, sailors from foreign countries, such as the

Chinese men pictured in document 3, experienced American foods on layovers in US ports. German foods were frowned upon in the United States, but Japanese Americans had the most difficulty maintaining culinary traditions during the war. The circumstances of the interment of over one hundred thousand Japanese and Japanese Americans prevented these people from accessing and cooking many of their traditional foods. The Japanese American children of the war generation grew up on government rations prepared in large cafeterias in the internment camps.

Following the war, food was at the heart of the Marshall Plan, which was central to US postwar policy in Europe. In document 5, the secretary of state, George C. Marshall, describes European hunger and justifies US aid in the region. Preventing starvation, and thereby fostering alliances, enabled the United States to remain influential, particularly in Western Europe. As new scientific data emerged in the 1940s and '50s, the US government began to make nutritional recommendations that encouraged consumers to incorporate a range of vegetables, fruits, and proteins into their daily diets. New technologies in food processing that were perfected during the war led to the adoption of convenience foods in many home kitchens during the 1950s. Faster, more innovative appliances were purchased for kitchens in suburban homes across the country. This large-scale consumerism even caught the eye of Soviet premier Nikita Khrushchev in his "kitchen debate" with US vice president Richard Nixon. A transcript of their 1959 discussion appears here as document 10.

DOCUMENT 1:

Freedom from Want, 1941

Source: Library of Congress, Prints and Photographs Division, reproduction #LC-USE6-D-002991.

Once Franklin Delano Roosevelt introduced the Four Freedoms they became a core component of wartime

Document 1

dialogue. Illustrations of the Four Freedoms appeared on textiles and in public displays. Popular artist Norman Rockwell's depictions of the Four Freedoms appeared in the widely circulated Saturday Evening Post. *A large family sitting down to a roast turkey dinner symbolized Rockwell's interpretation of freedom from want. In this image a woman is contemplating a photo montage of the Four Freedoms that was designed by artist Jean Carlu and displayed on the corner of Fourteenth Street and Pennsylvania Avenue in Washington, D.C., in November 1941 by the Office of Emergency Management. In it, freedom from want was conveyed through photos of a man eating a hot dog, a young girl drinking a glass of milk, an attractive arrangement of fruit at a grocer's, and shoppers making purchases at a dairy counter.*

Wartime Rationing, 1943

Source: War Ration Book Two, US Office of
Price Administration, Washington, DC.

*"Do with less so they'll have enough," urged a rationing
poster with an image of a US soldier drinking coffee. The
Office of Price Administration, which was part of the Office
of Emergency Management, was charged with establishing maximum prices for commodities and rationing
staples that were scarce so that everyone received a "fair
share." The Department of Agriculture handled sugar
rationing, and OPA managed the rationing of other foods,
as described in the leaflet below. The consumer pamphlet
below was included with Ration Book Two, which came
out in 1943. It explained why rationing was important
and how to use rationing points. Since each member of
a household was apportioned a certain number of ration
points, women buying for families had to be organized,
savvy shoppers to make the most efficient food purchases.*

Why Canned Fruits, Vegetables, and Soups are Rationed

Every week we are sending shiploads of canned goods to feed our
fighting men and our fighting allies in Africa, Britain, and the Pacific
islands. We must see that they get all the food they need. We at home
will share all that is left. Point Rationing will be used to guarantee you
and everyone a fair share of America's supply of canned and processed
fruits and vegetables, soups and juices.

How They Are Rationed

1. Every eligible man, woman, child and baby in the United States
is being given War Ration Book Two. (This book will not be used for
sugar or coffee.)

2. The BLUE stamps are for any kind of Canned or Bottled Fruits and Vegetables, Canned or Bottled Juices and Soups; Frozen Fruits and Vegetables; Dried Fruits. (The red stamps will be used later for meats.)

3. The stamps in this book are POINT stamps. The NUMBER on each stamp shows you how many points that stamp is worth.

4. The LETTERS show you WHEN to use the stamps. The year will be divided into rationing periods. You can use all BLUE stamps marked A, B, C in the first rationing period. A, B, and C stamps cannot be used after the first rationing period ends.

5. You must use the BLUE stamps when you buy ANY KIND of rationed processed foods. See the official list showing every kind of rationed processed food at your grocers. Different kinds of these foods will take different numbers of points. For example, a can of beans may take a different number of points from a can of peas.

> Rationed Foods
> Jars: Fruits, Vegetables, Soups, Juices
> Dried: Fruits
> Frozen: Fruits, Vegetables
> Bottled: Juices, Soups, Chili Sauce
> Canned: Fruits, Vegetables, Soups, Juices, Baby Foods

6. Of course, the more of anything you buy, the more points it will take. For example, a large can of peas will take more than a small one.

7. The Government will set the points for each kind and size and send out an Official Table of Point Values which your grocer must put up where you can see it. The Government will keep careful watch of the supply of these processed foods and make changes in point values from time to time, probably not oftener than once a month. The Government will announce these changes when it makes them and they will be put up in the stores.

8. The number of points for each kind of processed food will be THE SAME in ALL STORES and in all parts of the country.

Use Your OLD Ration Book for SUGAR and COFFEE.

How to Use Your New Ration Book To Buy
Canned or Bottled Fruits, Vegetables, Soups, and Juices;
Frozen Fruits and Vegetables; Dried Fruits

1. The Government has set the day when this rationing will start. On or before that day, take your War Ration Book with you when you go to buy any kind of processed foods.

2. Before you buy, find out how many points to give for the kind of processed foods you want. Prices do not set the points. The Government will set different points for each kind and size no matter what the price. Your grocer will put up the official list of points where you can see it. It will also be in the newspapers. *The points will not change just because the prices do.*

3. When you buy, take the right amount of blue stamps out of the book. Do this in front of your grocer or delivery man and hand them to him. The grocer must collect a ration stamp, or stamps, for all the rationed processed foods he sells. Every rationed processed food will take points as well as money.

4. Do not use more stamps than you need to make up the right amount. For example, if the food you buy calls for 13 stamps it is better to tear out an 8-point stamp and a 5-point stamp than two 5-point stamps and a 2 and a 1 point stamp. Save your smaller point stamps for lower point foods. You can take the stamps from more than one book belonging to your household if you need to.

5. Every person in your household including children of any age has a total of 48 points to use for all the processed foods for one ration period. This means that you may use ALL the blue stamps marked A, B, and C from all the books during the first period. You may use as many of the blue A, B, and C stamps as you wish at one time. *When they are used up you will not be able to buy any more of these processed foods till the next stamps are good.* The Government will announce the date when the next stamps are good.

6. Use your household's points carefully so that you will not run out of stamps. And buy with care to make your points come out even because the grocer will not be able to give you change in stamps. Use high-point stamps first, if you can.

IMPORTANT: You may use ALL the books of the household to

buy processed foods for the household. Anyone you wish can take the ration books to the store to do the buying for you or your household.

A Fair Share For All: We cannot afford to waste food or give some people more than their fair share. That is why canned fruits and vegetables are rationed and that is why meat is going to be rationed. Rationing of some foods is the best and fairest way to be sure that every American gets enough to eat.

DOCUMENT 3:

American Culinary Encounter, 1942

Source: Library of Congress, Prints and Photographs Division, reproduction #LC-USE6-D-006004.

Document 3

The war, which sprawled across several continents, enabled thousands of people who might not ordinarily have had opportunities to travel and encounter new cultures to sample new foods. The two Chinese seamen pictured in this photo worked on a British ship and were enjoying their first tastes of American food while on shore leave. They selected two of the most famous US products for their initial culinary encounter: a hot dog and a Coca-Cola.

DOCUMENT 4:

Eating in an Internment Camp, 1942

Source: *Topaz Times*, June 27, 1942.

President Roosevelt signed one of the most infamous executive orders of World War II in February 1942. E.O. 9066 ordered all Japanese and Japanese Americans living on the West Coast to be relocated to a series of government-maintained internment camps. The rationale was that the risk of Japanese acting as spies for their homeland was too great to ignore, even though the order did not include Hawaii. The camps were sprinkled throughout the West with some as far east as Arkansas. Internees had to relinquish their homes and businesses, sometimes losing significant financial assets, in order to move their families with little more than a suitcase or two to the camps. The camp at Topaz, in Utah, processed over eleven thousand people while it was open from September 1942 to October 1945. It functioned like a small city, and families at Topaz lived in barracks and children attended schools and played in recreation areas. Many of the camps raised cattle and poultry and cultivated large farms to help provide food for the war effort. When they could, internees planted small gardens outside of their barracks to supple-

ment their diets. Meals were served in dining halls and were made largely out of foods that came from a government warehouse. Parents, who might have preferred to preserve traditional Japanese foodways, saw their children regularly being served frankfurters. The camp newspaper, the Topaz Times, *ran a column called "The Kitchen" that documented aspects of the camp's food culture.*

Food for Babies

The baby formulae kitchen directed by Mrs. Harue Yamashita, registered nurse, is serving 350 tots from 1 to 3 years old. Infants under 1 year receive special formulae nourishment, including: eggs on Mondays, Wednesdays, Saturdays; and daily orange or tomato juice and individually treated milk. Incidentally, each of them will be given this week 6 cans of puree[d] food.

To all mothers who have not as yet done so, Mrs. Yamashita makes the request [that] they bring their babies to the Well-Baby Clinic at the Medical Center to have them weighed and to have formulae made for them by Dr. Eugenia Fujita. Dr. Fujita will also advise those mothers with children ready for cereal food.

The Amount We Eat

As an indication of the weekly ration of food . . . the commissary released the following list of foods received at the warehouse this week.

Cabbage 6000 lbs., carrots 4000 lbs., celery 2400 lbs., lettuce 180 crates, dry onions 4000 lbs., green onions 80 dozen, potatoes 160 sacks, white radishes 3000 lbs., tomatoes 3000 lbs., beets 2400 lbs., banana squash 2600 lbs., red radishes 80 dozen, bananas 100 lbs., grapefruit 90 boxes, oranges 90 boxes, watermelon 8000 lbs., cantaloupes 70 crates, eggs 120 crates, butter 960 lbs., cheese 500 lbs., beef carcass 22,000 lbs., mutton 4800 lbs., pork butts 2600 lbs., frankfurters 1850 lbs., bacon 1000 lbs., salt pork 720 lbs., assorted cold meats 100 lbs., sea bass 2200 lbs., rice 18,900 lbs. An average week's milk quota calls for 2170 gallons of bulk and 17,500 half-pint bottles.

This listing does not include the amount used for the special diet kitchens.

DOCUMENT 5:

George C. Marshall on Hunger in Europe, 1947

Source: "European Initiatives Essential to
Economic Recovery," *Department of State
Bulletin*, June 15, 1947, 1159–60.

*Tensions between the United States and the Soviet Union,
which had been an ally during the war, mounted once
the conflict came to a close. Joseph Stalin insisted on
maintaining a buffer zone in Eastern Europe between
Germany and his country while George Kennan's famous
"long telegram" in 1946 warned the Truman administration that the Soviet Union was looking to expand its
empire. Harry Truman's foreign policy doctrine aimed
to contain the spread of communism and offered aid to
any country that rebuffed communism, whether or not it
was democratic. In the summer of 1947, Secretary of State
George Marshall reported on his recent trip to Europe.
He worried about the continued deprivation and the lack
of economic development needed to provide basic food
staples. Ultimately, his call for aid to Europe launched
the Marshall Plan, which funneled billions of dollars to
rebuild infrastructure and help feed Europeans. Hungry
people might be more receptive to communist ideas and,
thus, the Marshall Plan also ensured that countries helped
by the US remained allies.*

I need not tell you gentlemen that the world situation is very serious. That must be apparent to all intelligent people. I think one difficulty is that the problem is one of such enormous complexity that the
very mass of facts presented to the public by press and radio make it
exceedingly difficult for the man in the street to reach a clear appraise-
ment of the situation. Furthermore, the people of this country are
distant from the troubled areas of the earth and it is hard for them to
comprehend the plight and consequent reactions of the long-suffering

peoples, and the effect of those reactions on their governments in connection with our efforts to promote peace in the world.

In considering the requirements for the rehabilitation of Europe, the physical loss of life, the visible destruction of cities, factories, mines, and railroads was correctly estimated, but it has become obvious during recent months that this visible destruction was probably less serious than the dislocation of the entire fabric of European economy. For the past ten years conditions have been highly abnormal. The feverish maintenance of the war effort engulfed all aspects of national economies. Machinery has fallen into disrepair or is entirely obsolete. Under the arbitrary and destructive Nazi rule, virtually every possible enterprise was geared into the German war machine. Longstanding commercial ties, private institutions, banks, insurance companies, and shipping companies disappeared, through loss of capital, absorption through nationalization, or by simple destruction. In many countries, confidence in the local currency has been severely shaken. The breakdown of the business structure of Europe during the war was complete. Recovery has been seriously retarded by the fact that two years after the close of hostilities a peace settlement with Germany and Austria has not been agreed upon. But even given a more prompt solution of these difficult problems, the rehabilitation of the economic structure of Europe quite evidently will require a much longer time and greater effort than had been foreseen.

There is a phase of this matter which is both interesting and serious. The farmer has always produced the foodstuffs to exchange with the city dweller for the other necessities of life. This division of labor is the basis of modern civilization. At the present time it is threatened with breakdown. The town and city industries are not producing adequate goods to exchange with the food-producing farmer. Raw materials and fuel are in short supply. Machinery is lacking or worn out. The farmer or the peasant cannot find the goods for sale which he desires to purchase. So the sale of his farm produce for money which he cannot use seems to him an unprofitable transaction. He, therefore, has withdrawn many fields from crop cultivation and is using them for grazing. He feeds more grain to stock and finds for himself and his family an ample supply of food, however short he may be on clothing and the other ordinary gadgets of civilization. Meanwhile people in the cities are short of food and fuel. So the governments are forced to use their foreign money and credits to procure these necessities abroad. This process exhausts funds which are urgently needed for reconstruction. Thus a very serious situation is rapidly developing which bodes no good for the world. The modern system of the division of labor upon which the exchange of products is based is in danger of breaking down.

The truth of the matter is that Europe's requirements for the next three or four years of foreign food and other essential products—principally from America—are so much greater than her present ability to pay that she must have substantial additional help or face economic, social, and political deterioration of a very grave character.

The remedy lies in breaking the vicious circle and restoring the confidence of the European people in the economic future of their own countries and of Europe as a whole. The manufacturer and the farmer throughout wide areas must be able and willing to exchange their products for currencies the continuing value of which is not open to question.

Aside from the demoralizing effect on the world at large and the possibilities of disturbances arising as a result of the desperation of the people concerned, the consequences to the economy of the United States should be apparent to all. It is logical that the United States should do whatever it is able to do to assist in the return of normal economic health in the world, without which there can be no political stability and no assured peace. Our policy is directed not against any country or doctrine but against hunger, poverty, desperation, and chaos. Its purpose should be the revival of a working economy in the world so as to permit the emergence of political and social conditions in which free institutions can exist. Such assistance, I am convinced, must not be on a piecemeal basis as various crises develop. Any assistance that this Government may render in the future should provide a cure rather than a mere palliative. Any government that is willing to assist in the task of recovery will find full cooperation, I am sure, on the part of the United States Government. Any government which maneuvers to block the recovery of other countries cannot expect help from us. Furthermore, governments, political parties, or groups which seek to perpetuate human misery in order to profit therefrom politically or otherwise will encounter the opposition of the United States.

It is already evident that, before the United States Government can proceed much further in its efforts to alleviate the situation and help start the European world on its way to recovery, there must be some agreement among the countries of Europe as to the requirements of the situation and the part those countries themselves will take in order to give proper effect to whatever action might be undertaken by this Government. It would be neither fitting nor efficacious for this Government to undertake to draw up unilaterally a program designed to place Europe on its feet economically. This is the business of the Europeans. The initiative, I think, must come from Europe. The role of this country should consist of friendly aid in the drafting of a European program and of later support of such a program so far as it may be practical for us to do so. The program should be a joint one, agreed to by a number, if not all, European nations.

An essential part of any successful action on the part of the United States is an understanding on the part of the people of America of the character of the problem and the remedies to be applied. Political passion and prejudice should have no part. With foresight, and a willingness on the part of our people to face up to the vast responsibility which history has clearly placed upon our country, the difficulties I have outlined can and will be overcome.

DOCUMENT 6:

Nutritional Recommendations, 1940s–1950s

Source: usda.gov

In 1943, the US Department of Agriculture introduced the "basic seven" food groups. The USDA had been offering nutritional advice since the early part of the century and was incorporating new information that was being discovered regarding vitamins and minerals that were important for health. During the war, the government had the additional motivation of trying to keep its workforce in good physical shape during the stress of mobilization. In 1956 the USDA revised recommendations, and the basic seven were slimmed down to the "basic four" food groups, which remained a standard for essential nutrition until the model was slightly revised in 1979, when a fifth group was included that encouraged people to moderate intake of fats, sugars, and alcohol.

USDA Chart explaining the Basic Seven:

For Health . . . eat some food from each group every day!

Group One: Green and Yellow Vegetables . . . some raw, some cooked, frozen or canned.

Group Two: Oranges, Tomatoes, Grapefruit . . . or raw cabbage or salad greens.

Group Three: Potatoes and Other Vegetables and Fruits . . . raw, dried, cooked, frozen or canned.

Group Four: Milk and Milk Products . . . fluid, evaporated, dried milk or cheese.

Group Five: Meat, Poultry, Fish or Eggs . . . or dried beans, peas, nuts, or peanut butter.

Group Six: Bread Flour and Cereals . . . Natural, whole grain or enriched or restored.

Group Seven: Butter and Fortified Margarine (with added vitamin A).

In addition to the Basic Seven . . . eat any other foods you want.

USDA Chart with Serving Examples:

A Day's Pattern for Good Eating from the Basic Seven

Breakfast: Fruit, Cereal with Milk, Bread, Butter (or fortified margarine), Beverage.

Lunch or Supper: Meat, Poultry, Fish, Eggs, Cheese (Main Dish or Sandwich); Vegetable—cooked or raw, green or yellow; Bread; Butter (or fortified margarine); Fruit; Milk.

Dinner: Meat, Poultry, Fish, Eggs, Cheese; Potato; Vegetable; Salad; Bread; Butter (or fortified margarine); Dessert; Beverage.

USDA "A Guide to Good Eating"

Milk: 2 or more glasses daily . . . for adults. 3 or 4 glasses daily . . . for children to drink combined with other foods, in ice cream and in cheese.

Vegetables: 2 or more servings daily other than potato . . . one green or yellow, "greens" often.

Fruits: 2 or more servings a day . . . at least one raw; citrus fruit or tomato daily.

Eggs: 3 to 5 a week; 1 daily preferred.

Meat, Cheese, Fish, Poultry: 1 or more servings daily . . . dried beans, peas, peanuts occasionally.

Cereal and Bread: 2 or more servings daily . . . whole grain value or enriched, added milk improves nutritional values.

Butter: 2 or more tablespoons daily.

"Food for Fitness: A Daily Food Guide [Basic Four]"

Milk Group: Some milk for everyone: Children under 9 . . . 2 to 3 cups; Children 9–12 . . . 3 or more cups; Teenagers . . . 4 or more cups; Adults . . . 2 or more cups.

Meat Group: 2 or more servings . . . beef, veal, pork, lamb, poultry, fish, eggs. As alternates: dry beans, dry peas, nuts.

Vegetable Fruit Group: 4 or more servings. Include: A citrus fruit or other fruit or vegetable—important for vitamin C. A dark-green or deep yellow vegetable for vitamin A—at least every other day. Other vegetables and fruits including potatoes.

Bread Cereal Group: 4 or more servings . . . whole grain, enriched or restored.

DOCUMENT 7:

New Appliances, 1950s

Source: Library of Congress, Prints and
Photographs Division, reproduction
#LC-USE6-D-003456.

The consumer economy in the US boomed in the postwar years. As men returned from the theaters of war, many of them married and settled down in houses in newly built suburbs like Levittown on Long Island, New York. Because many consumer goods had not been widely available during the war, production lines hummed as they now turned out new kitchen appliances and other commodities. Hotpoint, for example, had been making electric appliances since the early twentieth century and developed a refrigerator with wheels, for easier cleaning, in the early 1950s. The woman in the photo below care-

Document 7

fully places a pot into her large capacity refrigerator. The contents of her refrigerator show that, like many women, she employed a combination of fresh ingredients and convenience foods in her cooking.

DOCUMENT 8:

Condiment Production

Source: Library of Congress, Prints and Photographs Division, reproduction #LC-D420–2782 DLC.

Convenience foods became increasingly common after World War II in part because of new techniques in food preservation that were developed to supply troops

Document 8

*around the world. After the war, companies began mar-
keting these new foods to home cooks. Packaged foods,
such as boxed cake mixes, now gave women a choice as to
whether they wanted to bake a cake from scratch or save
time and use a mix. Frozen foods proliferated in the 1950s
since experiments with freezing food staples like orange
juice during the war had improved the integrity of frozen
foods. Swanson introduced entire frozen dinners with a
meat and side dishes that became known as "TV dinners"
since families were increasingly eating dinner in front of
their new televisions. Frozen fish sticks, which came out
in the early 1950s, also proved to be very popular with
families. Housewives now rarely took the time to make
condiments from scratch since they were readily available
for purchase. In this image, workers check the quality of
ketchup that will probably soon be purchased for a family's dinner from the aisles of a supermarket.*

DOCUMENT 9:

Convenience Food Recipes, 1950s

Source: Recipes courtesy of Lizabeth Foster.

*Bonnie Sealey had to get dinner on the table for a family
of four each night in their Seattle home in the late 1950s.
Like many women at that time, she worked full time and
turned to recipes that were reliable and uncomplicated
when she got home from the middle school where she was
a secretary. Convenience foods, such as frozen vegetables
and canned condensed soup, were marketed to women,
like Bonnie, who used them to feed a home-cooked meal
to their husbands and children after work and school.
Many wives and mothers, however, did not rely exclusively
on convenience foods because they took pleasure in dedi-*

cating time and love to nourishing their families. On the weekend, for example, Bonnie would sometimes simmer a tomato sauce on the stove all day that her children could smell down the street while playing. Alternatively, she might select a recipe from her Betty Crocker Cookbook or slow cook some corned beef and cabbage or a pork roast with all of the trimmings on Sunday afternoons. Yet on weeknights, she often took advantage of recipes with convenience foods that were accessible, laborsaving, and cost effective for working families. Her recipes were typed on note cards with some handwritten annotations. The examples below have been duplicated as she wrote them.

Chicken Casserole

1 whole chicken

1 can cream of mushroom soup

1 can cream of chicken soup

8 oz. sour cream

1 stack pkg. Ritz crackers

1½ stick oleo

Cook chicken and de-bone. Place in 2 qt. casserole dish. Mix sour cream with soups and pour over chicken. Crush crackers and put over soup mixture. Melt butter and pour over crackers. Bake at 350 degrees for 30 min.

Porcupine Meatballs

1# ground beef

½ cup rice (uncooked)

2 cans tomato sauce w/2 cans water

1 tsp. salt

Combine meat, rice, salt and ½ can sauce. Make small meatballs. Place in casserole, add the remaining 1½ cans tomato sauce and water to cover meatballs. Add a tad of sugar and salt to this, cover and bake 350° 1 hour—uncovered for last 30 minutes.

Sausage and Broccoli Casserole

Cook 1# links. Cut into small pieces. Drain. Cook 10 oz. pkg. frz. broccoli. Drain. Place broccoli in a lightly greased 1½ qt. casserole.

Combine: Sausage, 3 Tbls. chopped green pepper, 2 Tbls. chopped onion, 3 Tbls. minced parsley, 2 Tbls. flour. Mix well.

Spoon ½ mixture over broccoli. Top w/3 hard boiled eggs, sliced. Spoon remaining mixture over eggs. Combine 10¾ oz. can mushroom soup undiluted and ⅓ cup milk. Pour over casserole.

Combine ½ cup dry breadcrumbs and 3 Tbls. melted butter and sprinkle over casserole. Bake 375°—30 min. Serve over hot rice.

DOCUMENT 10:

Kitchen Debate, 1959

Sources: *New York Times*, July 25, 1959; and CIA Freedom of Information Act Electronic Reading Room.

In the late 1950s, the Cold War between the United States and the Soviet Union thawed after Nikita Khrushchev came to power and denounced Joseph Stalin's violent extremism in 1956. In 1958 and '59 the two rivals embarked on a cultural exchange in which national exhibitions exposed citizens to life in their adversary's country. When Vice President Richard Nixon visited the American installation in Moscow with Premier Khrushchev on July 24, 1959, an informal debate over capitalist production of consumer goods ensued in a model kitchen. Although the "kitchen debate" was largely convivial, Khrushchev seemed to doubt the utility of many new American appliances. The New York Times *quoted Khrushchev jesting during this exchange: "Don't you have a machine that puts food into the mouth and pushes it down? Many things you've shown us are interesting but they are not needed in life. They have no useful purpose. They are merely gadgets." The* Times *account said they were referencing a washing machine, not a dishwasher, at the beginning of the conversation. A washing machine can be seen in the model kitchen in photos of their exchange; however, automatic dishwashers were also being widely installed in new homes at this time.*

NIXON. I want to show you this kitchen. It is like those of our houses in California. (*Nixon points to dishwasher.*)

KHRUSHCHEV. We have such things.

NIXON. This is our newest model. This is the kind which is built in thousands of units for direct installations in the houses. In America, we like to make life easier for women. . . .

KHRUSHCHEV. Your capitalistic attitude toward women does not occur under Communism.

NIXON. I think that this attitude towards women is universal. What we want to do is make life more easy for our housewives. . . . This house can be bought for $14,000, and most [World War II] veterans can buy a home in the bracket of $10,000 to $15,000. Let me give you an example that you can appreciate. Our steel workers as you know are now on strike. But any steel worker could buy this house. They earn $3 an hour. This house costs about $100 a month to buy on a contract running 25 to 30 years.

KHRUSHCHEV. We have steel workers and peasants who can afford to spend $14,000 for a house. Your American houses are built to last only 20 years so builders could sell new houses at the end. We build firmly. We build for our children and grandchildren.

NIXON. American houses last for more than 20 years, but, even so, after 20 years, many Americans want a new house or a new kitchen. Their kitchen is obsolete by that time. The American system is designed to take advantage of new inventions and new techniques.

KHRUSHCHEV. This theory does not hold water. Some things never get out of date—furniture and furnishings—perhaps, but not houses. I have read much about America and American houses and I do not think that this exhibit and what you say is strictly accurate. . . .

KHRUSHCHEV. I hope I have not insulted you.

NIXON. I have been insulted by experts. Everything we say is in good humor. . . .

KHRUSHCHEV. The Americans have created their own image of the Soviet man. But he is not as you think. You think the Russian people will be dumbfounded to see these things but the fact is that newly built Russian houses have all this equipment right now. . . .

KHRUSHCHEV. In Russia, all you have to do to get a house is to be born in the Soviet Union. You are entitled to housing. . . . In America, if you don't have a dollar, you [have] a right to choose between sleeping in a house or on the pavement. Yet you say we are the slave to Communism.

NIXON. I appreciate that you are very articulate and energetic.

KHRUSHCHEV. Energetic is not the same thing as wise.

NIXON. If you were in the Senate, we would call you a filibusterer! You do all the talking and don't let anyone else talk. This exhibit was not designed to astound but to interest. Diversity, the right to choose, the fact that we have 1,000 builders building 1,000 different houses is the most important thing. We don't have one decision made at the top by one government official. This is the difference.

KHRUSHCHEV. On politics, we will never agree with you. For instance, Mikoyan [probably Anastas Mikoyan, a prominent Soviet politician] likes very peppery soup. I do not. But this does not mean that we do not get along.

NIXON. You can learn from us, and we can learn from you. There must be a free exchange. Let the people choose the kind of house, the kind of soup, the kind of ideas they want.

CHAPTER 10

Politics, Protest, and Food

The decade of the 1960s brought change to many quarters across the United States. The student-driven sit-in movement, which began in February 1960, demonstrated that momentum for civil rights legislation was on the rise. This movement dramatically illustrated the injustice of racial segregation by highlighting lunch counters in department stores like Woolworth and Kress. African Americans were welcome to spend money in the stores; however, they were banned from dining at the public counters. Food establishments like restaurants, cafeterias, and lunch counters were an important locus of struggle in the campaign to dismantle segregation as they focused on the essential right to eat in a public facility. Document 1 is a court ruling that mandated the desegregation of a cafeteria at the Arkansas State Capitol in compliance with the Civil Rights Act of 1964, which outlawed discrimination in public accommodations.

Direct-action nonviolence, as waged by leaders like Martin Luther King Jr. and the Southern Christian Leadership Conference, was one facet of a wide range of movements throughout the 1960s. Campaigns for women's rights and gay rights as well as the anti-Vietnam movement blazed new trails. Food was also at the center of the migrant worker's labor movement in California. Activist Cesar Chavez, also a proponent of nonviolence, utilized the philosophy in his fight on behalf of the workers who picked farm goods that were vital to American palates. Radical groups that emerged in cities like Berkeley in the late 1960s focused on creating a counterculture. Communalism and vegetarianism were values that spread among some communities through the 1970s. For example, as document 3 reveals, the Diggers wanted to forge a free society in which staple foods were easily accessible to all people regardless of class.

Food also played an important role in the halls of government during this era, and documents in this chapter record White House menus, reveal contemporary anxieties about food habits, and demonstrate that food practices could be used as a tool in foreign diplomacy. Food was emphasized in the Kennedy White House under the direction of First Lady Jacqueline Kennedy. For the first time, the White House employed a French chef to prepare state dinners, lunches, and teas for important visitors. The elegant food was the centerpiece of the glamorous aesthetic that the young, handsome family brought to Pennsylvania Avenue. The government also took notice of food in the early 1970s when diet fads were marketed widely and becoming increasingly popular. While obesity was a vital issue, a US Senate committee on nutrition worried that fly-by-night diet schemes could be dangerous to the public. When President Richard Nixon famously journeyed to China to help mend diplomatic ties, he and his wife were honored at many elaborate banquets where they encountered unfamiliar dishes. The toasts given at these dinners were crucial to solidifying good will with the Chinese. When food becomes political, every bite off of the chopsticks becomes a moment that could either charm or offend a foreign host.

DOCUMENT 1:

Desegregating Eating Establishments in Arkansas, 1960s

Source: *Ozell Sutton v. Capitol Club, Inc.*, US District Court, Eastern District, Arkansas, Western Division, No. LR-64-C-124, April 12, 1965.

In order to circumvent the Civil Rights Act of 1964, which mandated the desegregation of public facilities, the cafeteria inside the Arkansas State Capitol reorganized as a private club and refused to serve black citizens. Members of the civil rights organization the Student Nonviolent Coordinating Committee attempted to integrate the facility on several occasions but were turned back by state troopers using tear gas and billy clubs. Civil rights activist Ozell Sutton, then working as assistant director of the Arkansas Council on Human Relations, successfully sued the managers of the cafeteria for operating on a segregated basis. The document below is the US District Court's ruling.

Ozell SUTTON v. CAPITOL CLUB, INC.

United States District Court, Eastern District, Arkansas, Western Division, No. LR-64-C-124, April 12, 1965, F——Supp.——

HENLEY, District Judge

MEMORANDUM OPINION

Ozell Sutton, a Negro citizen of Arkansas, has brought this suit in equity to put an end to alleged racial discrimination in the cafeteria facilities located in the basement of the Arkansas State Capitol. The defendant, Capitol Club, Inc., an Arkansas non-profit corporation, holds a lease on the facilities executed in July 1964 by the so-called Capitol Building Commission. . . .

The case has been tried to the Court, and this memorandum opinion incorporates the Court's Findings of Fact and Conclusions of Law.

Prior to the organization of the defendant corporation on July 21, 1964, the cafeteria in the Capitol had been operated for a number of years by Mrs. S. E. Tyer under lease from the Commission. The Court finds from a preponderance of the evidence that while the cafeteria may have been patronized primarily by State employees it was in fact a public eating accommodation. The Court further finds from a preponderance of the evidence that Negroes were not served in the cafeteria, and that their exclusion therefrom was on account of their race.

The Civil Rights Act of 1964 became effective on July 2 of that year. On July 15 plaintiff was at the Capitol on business and about lunch time he entered the cafeteria seeking service. He was advised by Mrs. Tyer that notwithstanding the passage of the Act, the cafeteria did not propose to serve Negroes until the Act had been tested in and construed by the courts.

On July 21, 1964, Clarence R. Thornbrough, the Executive Secretary to the Governor, and six other State employees, proceeding under Act

176 of 1963, brought about the incorporation of the defendant as a private club. On the same day Mrs. Tyer surrendered her lease to the cafeteria, and a new lease, which seems to be identical in terms to Mrs. Tyer's lease, was executed by the Commission in favor of the defendant corporation. Mrs. Tyer remained in the management of the cafeteria. She was not compensated for her lease, and she continued to use in the operation of the cafeteria her own utensils and equipment just as she had before the surrender of her lease.

The operation of the cafeteria continued from July 21, 1964, until later in March of the current year when it was closed following racial demonstrations which produced some violence.

It is the theory of the plaintiff that defendant corporation is not a bona fide private club: that both before and after defendant's incorporation the cafeteria was operated as a public accommodation; that racial segregation was practiced in the cafeteria prior to the defendant's incorporation and has been continued since; and that the alleged discriminatory operation of the facility is violative both of the Fourteenth Amendment to the Constitution of the United States and of the public accommodations provisions of the 1964 Civil Rights Act.

In defending the case the defendant asserts that it is a bona fide private club; that it is operating the cafeteria as such; that its operation is not State action within the purview of the Fourteenth Amendment; that its operation is in fact racially non-discriminatory; and that in any event it is as a private club exempt from the relevant provisions of the Act. . . .

The Court does not believe that a detailed discussion of the facts or of the evidence is necessary or that such a discussion would be particularly helpful. While Capitol Club, Inc. was organized for the ostensible purpose of promoting the convenience of State employees in obtaining meals in the cafeteria more expeditiously than would he possible in a facility open to the general public, the Court finds from the record as a whole that following the defendant's incorporation and take-over of the cafeteria, the operation of that facility continued essentially as it had before. That is to say, before Capitol Club, Inc. was organized the cafeteria was a public eating place in a public building from which facilities Negroes were excluded on account of their race, and the Court is convinced that after the organization of the Club the cafeteria continued to be a public eating place with its patrons not in fact limited to Club members and their guests, and that the cafeteria under Club management continued to exclude Negroes on account of their race just as had been done when Mrs. Tyer was operating the cafeteria on her own account.

Prior to the passage of the Civil Rights Act of 1964 it had become established that the Equal Protection Clause of the Fourteenth Amendment prohibited a State or municipality from operating on State or municipally owned property a public restaurant, cafe, or cafeteria from which would-be patrons were excluded on account of their race or in which patrons were segregated on the basis of race; and that prohibition extended to the operation of such a facility by a private individual or corporation. . . .

The Court's conclusion that defendant's operation of a public cafeteria from which Negroes were excluded on account of their race constituted a violation of the Fourteenth Amendment renders it unnecessary to determine whether that operation was also a violation of the Public Accommodations Sections of the Civil Rights Act.

A decree will be entered enjoining the defendant from any resumption of the activities which the Court has found to be unconstitutional.

Dated this 12th day of April, 1965.

DOCUMENT 2:

Cesar Chavez and the United Farm Workers, 1960s

Source: The White House, Office of the Press Secretary, October 8, 2012.

Mexican American Cesar Chavez was born into an Arizona family who owned a small farm. During the Great Depression, his family, like many families in the 1930s, was forced to uproot and head for California, where they aimed to find jobs as farm workers. In 1965, grape workers in Delano went on strike to protest wage cuts during the harvest season, and Chavez became their leader. Chavez

*creatively utilized a variety of tactics, including fasting,
following the example of Gandhi, and calling on people
across the nation to stop buying grapes. Chavez appealed
to the California Grape and Fruit Tree League as human
beings in his famous "Letter from Delano." "We do not
hate you," Chavez assured the growers; "we hate the agri-
business system that keeps us enslaved." The ensuing grape
boycott led to new contracts for the workers and the establishment of the United Farm Workers' Union. In the 2012
speech below, President Barack Obama honors Chavez
by dedicating to his movement a national monument in
Keene, California.*

THE PRESIDENT. Good morning! Buenos dias! (*Applause.*) Si, se
puede! (*Applause.*) Thank you. Thank you so much.

AUDIENCE. Four more years! Four more years! Four more years!

THE PRESIDENT. Thank you, everybody. Thank you so much. I am
truly grateful to be here. It is such a great honor to be with you
on this beautiful day, a day that has been a long time coming.

To the members of the Chavez family and those who knew and
loved Cesar; to the men and women who've worked so hard for
so long to preserve this place—I want to say to all of you, thank
you. Your dedication, your perseverance made this day possible.

I want to acknowledge the members of my administration who have
championed this project from the very beginning—Secretary
Ken Salazar, Secretary Hilda Solis, Nancy Sutley. (*Applause.*)
To Governor Brown, Mayor Villaraigosa—(*Applause.*)—
Congressman Grijalva—they are here. We are grateful for your
presence. And I also want to recognize my dear friend, somebody
we're so proud of—Arturo Rodriguez, the current president of
the UFW. (*Applause.*)

Most of all, I want to thank Helen Chavez. (*Applause.*) In the
years to come, generations of Americans will stand where we
stand and see a piece of history—a tribute to a great man and
a great movement. But to Helen, this will always be home. It's
where she fought alongside the man that she loved; where she

raised eight children and spoiled 31 grandchildren and 15 great-grandchildren. (*Applause.*) This is where she continues to live out the rest of her days.

So, Helen, today we are your guests. We appreciate your hospitality, and you should feel free to kick us out whenever you want. (Laughter.)

Today, La Paz joins a long line of national monuments—stretching from the Statue of Liberty to the Grand Canyon—monuments that tell the story of who we are as Americans. It's a story of natural wonders and modern marvels; of fierce battles and quiet progress. But it's also a story of people—of determined, fearless, hopeful people who have always been willing to devote their lives to making this country a little more just and a little more free.

One of those people lies here, beneath a rose garden at the foot of a hill he used to climb to watch the sun rise. And so today we celebrate Cesar Chavez. (*Applause.*)

Cesar would be the first to say that this is not a monument to one man. The movement he helped to lead was sustained by a generation of organizers who stood up and spoke out, and urged others to do the same—including the great Dolores Huerta, who is here today. (*Applause.*)

It drew strength from Americans of every race and every background who marched and boycotted together on behalf of "La Causa." And it was always inspired by the farm workers themselves, some of whom are with us. This place belongs to you, too.

But the truth is we would not be here if it weren't for Cesar. Growing up as the son of migrant workers who had lost their home in the Great Depression, Cesar wasn't easy on his parents. He described himself as "caprichoso"—(*laughter*)—capricious. His brother Richard had another word for him—(*Applause.*)—stubborn.

By the time he reached 7th grade, Cesar estimated he had attended 65 elementary schools, following the crop cycles with his family, working odd jobs, sometimes living in roadside tents without electricity or plumbing. It wasn't an easy childhood. But Caesar always was different. While other kids could identify all the hottest cars, he memorized the names of labor leaders and politicians.

After serving in the Navy during World War II, Cesar returned to the fields. And it was a time of great change in America, but too often that change was only framed in terms of war and peace, black and white, young and old. No one seemed to care about the invisible farm workers who picked the nation's food—bent down in the beating sun, living in poverty, cheated by growers, abandoned in old age, unable to demand even the most basic rights.

But Cesar cared. And in his own peaceful, eloquent way, he made other people care, too. A march that started in Delano with a handful of activists—(*Applause.*)—that march ended 300 miles away in Sacramento with a crowd 10,000 strong. (*Applause.*) A boycott of table grapes that began in California eventually drew 17 million supporters across the country, forcing growers to agree to some of the first farm worker contracts in history. Where there had once been despair, Cesar gave workers a reason to hope. "What [the growers] don't know," he said, "is that it's not bananas or grapes or lettuce. It's people."

It's people. More than higher wages or better working conditions, that was Cesar's gift to us—a reminder that we are all God's children, that every life has value, that, in the words of one of his heroes, Dr. King, "we are caught in an inescapable network of mutuality, tied in a single garment of destiny."

Cesar didn't believe in helping those who refused to help themselves, but he did believe that when someone who works 12 hours a day in the fields can earn enough to put food on the table and maybe save up enough to buy a home, that that makes our communities stronger, that lifts up our entire economy.

He believed that when a worker is treated fairly and humanely by their employer that adds meaning to the values this country was founded upon, and credence to the claim that out of many, we are one. And he believed that when a child anywhere in America can dream beyond her circumstances and work to realize that dream, it makes all our futures just a little bit brighter. (*Applause.*)

It was that vision, that belief in the power of opportunity that drove Cesar every day of his life. It's a vision that says, maybe I never had a chance to get a good education, but I want my daughter to go to college. Maybe I started out working in the fields, but someday I'll own my own business. Maybe I have to make sacrifices, but those sacrifices are worth it if it means a better life for my family.

That's the story of my ancestors; that's the story of your ancestors. It's the promise that has attracted generations of immigrants to our shores from every corner of the globe, sometimes at great risk, drawn by the idea that no matter who you are, or what you look like, or where you come from, this is the place where you can make it if you try. (*Applause.*)

Today, we have more work to do to fulfill that promise. The recession we're fighting our way back from is still taking a toll, especially in Latino communities, which already faced higher unemployment and poverty rates. Even with the strides we've made, too many workers are still being denied basic rights and simple respect. But thanks to the strength and character of the American people, we are making progress. Our businesses are creating more jobs. More Americans are getting back to work.

And even though we have a difficult road ahead, I know we can keep moving forward together. (*Applause.*) I know it because Cesar himself worked for 20 years as an organizer without a single major victory—think about that—but he refused to give up. He refused to scale back his dreams. He just kept fasting and marching and speaking out, confident that his day would come.

And when it finally did, he still wasn't satisfied. After the struggle for higher wages, Cesar pushed for fresh drinking water and worker's compensation, for pension plans and safety from pesticides—always moving, always striving for the America he knew we could be.

More than anything, that's what I hope our children and grandchildren will take away from this place. Every time somebody's son or daughter comes and learns about the history of this movement, I want them to know that our journey is never hopeless, our work is never done. I want them to learn about a small man guided by enormous faith—in a righteous cause, a loving God, the dignity of every human being. I want them to remember that true courage is revealed when the night is darkest and the resistance is strongest and we somehow find it within ourselves to stand up for what we believe in. (*Applause.*)

Cesar once wrote a prayer for the farm workers that ends with these words:

Let the Spirit flourish and grow,

So that we will never tire of the struggle.

Let us remember those who have died for justice,

For they have given us life.

Help us love even those who hate,

So we can change the world. (*Applause.*)

Our world is a better place because Cesar Chavez decided to change it. Let us honor his memory. But most importantly, let's live up to his example. (*Applause.*)

Thank you. God bless you. (*Applause.*) God bless America. Si, se puede! (*Applause.*)

AUDIENCE. Si, se puede! (*Applause.*)

THE PRESIDENT. Si, se puede. (*Applause.*)

AUDIENCE. Si, se puede! (*Applause.*)

THE PRESIDENT. Thank you, everybody. (*Applause.*)

DOCUMENT 3:

The Diggers' Free City, 1968

Source: *The Digger Papers,* August 1968, 15.

The Diggers were a street theater group in the Haight Ashbury neighborhood in San Francisco in the late 1960s. They emerged from the counterculture movement and were inspired by civil rights campaigns as well as the

bohemian art scene of the era. A main part of their anar-
chist social agenda was creating a free city. Toward that
end, they distributed free food in the park and opened free
stores where a loose coalition of volunteers oversaw the
distribution of donated goods and some food staples. They
also became known for their home-baked whole-wheat
bread that was available at their free bakery. The Diggers
were on the cusp of the natural foods movement that blos-
somed in places like Berkeley in the late 1960s and '70s. As
the Vietnam War wound down, many antiwar protestors
and other activists began to focus on concerns closer to
home. As the personal became political, youthful hippies
who were critical of consumer culture moved to communes
and learned to grow and cook their own food. The excerpt
below explains the idea of the free city and how it applied
to food distribution.

The Post-Competitive, Comparative Game of a Free City

Our state of awareness demands that we uplift our efforts from competitive game playing in the underground to the comparative roles of
free families in *free cities.*

We must pool our resource and interact our energies to provide
the freedom for our individual activities.

In each city of the world there is a loose competitive underground
composed of groups whose aims overlap, conflict, and generally ener-
vate the desired goal of autonomy. By now we all have guns, know
how to use them, know our enemy, and are ready to defend. We know
that we ain't gonna take no more shit. So it's about time we carried
ourselves a little heavier and got down to the business of creating free
cities within the urban environments of the western world.

Free Cities are composed of Free Families (e.g. in San Francisco:
Diggers, Black Panthers, Provos, Mission Rebels and various revolu-
tionist gangs and communes) who establish and maintain services
that provide a base of freedom for autonomous groups to carry out
their programs without having to hassle for food, printing facilities,

transportation, mechanics, money, housing, working space, clothes, machinery, trucks, etc.

At this point in our revolution it is demanded that the families, communes, black organizations and gangs of every city in America co-ordinate and develop Free Cities where everything that is necessary can be obtained for free by those involved in the various activities of the individual clans.

Every brother should have what he needs to do his thing.

Free City:

An outline . . . a beginning
Each service should be performed by a tight
gang of brothers whose commitment should enable
them to handle an overload of work with ability
and enthusiasm. 'Tripsters' soon get bored, hopefully
Before they cause an economic strain. . . .

Free Food Storage and Distribution Center

[Volunteers] should hit every available source of free food—produce markets, farmer's markets, meat packing plants, farms, dairies, sheep and cattle ranches, agricultural colleges, and giant institutions (for the uneaten vats of food)—and fill up their trucks with the surplus by begging, borrowing, stealing, forming liaisons and communications with delivery drivers for the left-overs from their routes . . . [and the] best method is to work in two shifts: morning group picks up the foodstuffs and the afternoon shift delivers it to the list of Free Families and the poor peoples of the ghettoes. everyday. Hard work.

This gang should help people pool their welfare food stamps and get their old ladies or a group to open a free restaurant for people on the move and those who live on the streets. Giant scores should be stored in a garage-type warehouse equipped with freezers and its whereabouts known only to the Free Food Gang. This group should also set up and provide help for canning, preserving, bread baking, and feasts and anything and everything else that has to do with food.

DOCUMENT 4:

Menus from the Kennedy and Johnson White Houses, 1962 and 1964

Sources: "Jacqueline Kennedy Entertains: The Art of the White House Dinner," John F. Kennedy Presidential Library and Museum; National Museum of American History, The First Ladies at the Smithsonian, *Washington Post*, February 3, 2011.

The Kennedy-Johnson ticket in 1960 brought together two distinct strands of the Democratic Party. Kennedy, an Ivy Leaguer from a moneyed family, represented the liberal Northeast, while Johnson had attended Southwest Texas Teacher's College and clawed his way to the US Senate in the rough-and-tumble world of southern politics. John F. Kennedy and Lyndon B. Johnson were both iconic leaders during the turbulent 1960s but approached the presidency with divergent strategies, styles of management, and tastes. The Kennedy years ushered in the decade with a great deal of promise and hoopla. The "Camelot" label that is often attached to the Kennedy White House connotes the fine décor and refined elegance that graced the executive mansion while it was occupied by the fine-looking New England family. On the other hand, Johnson cultivated an image as a no-nonsense Texan, vacationed at his ranch, and was well known for his straightforward, unbending powers of persuasion. Perhaps nowhere were their diverse cultural predilections more apparent than in the menus for events during their administrations. According to the JFK Library, 43 dinners, 113 luncheons and 34 receptions were held during the Kennedy years from 1961 to 1963. Jacqueline Kennedy hired French chef René Verdon to head the White House kitchen, a decision that reflected the influence of French cuisine in the United States and that was epitomized by the popularization of Julia Child's

Mastering the Art of French Cooking *in the early 1960s. Prior to Verdon's tenure, the White House kitchen had been managed mainly by caterers and navy stewards. When the Johnson family inherited the White House, tastes changed significantly. Down-home southern fare took precedent over European sophistication. Verdon left the White House in 1965, reportedly after Lady Bird Johnson hired a food coordinator who cut costs by stocking the pantry with canned and frozen vegetables. The Washington Post wrote that Verdon further objected to serving "barbecued spare ribs" to "ladies in white gloves." The second menu below, created while Verdon was still at the White House, brought a French flair to what was essentially meat and potatoes. The dessert must have been tailored for U Thant, the secretary general of the United Nations.*

Kennedy Dinner

Inglenook Pinot Chardonnay – Aspic of Salmon Dorian, Sauce Vincent

Chateau Haut-Brion, 1955 – Roast Spring Lamb, Rice a la Orientale, Spinach a la crème

Green Salad, Brie Cheese

Piper Heidsieck, 1955 – Bombe glace aux peches, Petit-fours sec

The White House, Monday, June 3, 1963

Johnson Dinner

Pinot Chardonnay, 1962 – Crabmeat Surprise

Charles King Cabernet Sauvignon, 1959 – Chateaubriand White House, Dauphine potatoes, Puree Favorite

Green Salad, Port-du-Salut Cheese

Blanc de Blancs, 1959 – Coppelia U Thant

The White House, Thursday, August 6, 1964

DOCUMENT 5:

Nixon in China, 1972

Sources: Menu from Dinner Given during President Nixon's Visit to Peking, China, 02/25/1972, National Archives and Records Administration. Toast Proposed by Prime Minister Chou En-Lai, NSC Files, Richard Nixon Presidential Library and Museum, Yorba Linda, CA. Toast Proposed by Richard Nixon, February 1972, NSC Files, Richard Nixon Presidential Library and Museum.

President Nixon's policy of détente, or cooperation, with Communist countries inaugurated an important new era of international stability during the Cold War. When Nixon visited China in the early 1970s, the United States had not maintained diplomatic relations with the Chinese since the Communists had created the People's Republic after triumphing in a civil war in the late 1940s. The rapport forged by Richard Nixon and Henry Kissinger paved the way for increased trade between the United States and China and full diplomatic relations were established in 1979. China was soon to occupy a seat in the United Nations. Adhering to protocol and embracing the customs of this foreign culture were paramount when Nixon spent a week in China in the winter of 1972. This included the realm of food. Images of the journey show Nixon using chopsticks even if he sometimes puzzled over the food being served. The banquets on the trip were significant events that offered an opportunity for vital cultural exchange outside the arena of formal diplomatic talks. (Several of the translators who were very busy on this trip were women, and Nixon offered a toast to "true women.")

Menu from Banquet during Nixon's Visit to China

Hors d'Oeuvre
Four Treasures of Duck
Fried Giblets
Roast Duck
Mushrooms and Sprouts
Duck Bone Soup
Lotus Seeds Sweet Porridge
Fruits

Toast Proposed by Prime Minister Chou En-Lai at Banquet, February 24, 1972

Mr. President and Mrs. Nixon, friends from the United States and Comrades.

Today we have both a working dinner and a resting dinner here. So there is no need for me to say anything about the political aspect and I would like to change the topic. I would like to read half of a poem written by Chairman Mao when we reached a mountain called Liupan Shan, a mountain in the northern part of Szechuan Province. It was written at the mountain in September 1935.

> The sky is high, the clouds are pale.
> We watch the wild geese flying south till they vanish.
> We count the two thousand miles we have come already.
> If we reach not the Great Wall we are not true men.

. . . And you have all gone to the Great Wall today, so you have all become true men. For this I would like to propose a toast on the occasion of your reaching the Great Wall and becoming true men.

Toast Proposed by President Nixon at Banquet, February 24, 1972

Mr. Prime Minister and all of your distinguished guests tonight.

It is very difficult for me to express in words our appreciation for the hospitality reflected by this banquet and also to express our appreciation for the welcome that we have received in the days that we have been here in Peking. As we look back on these days, it seems that our only regret is that we could not be here longer. . . .

I want to say we had a great experience when we did reach the Great Wall. And as I rode in the car with the Vice Premier, I realized that we had come a long way to reach the Great Wall. . . . A wall can protect us, or a wall can divide us, and we believe that this new relationship that we have begun with this meeting will help to protect us and not divide us. Because the division in the world is what creates the great problems in the world, and we hope that in the years ahead people all over the world will have the opportunity we had today: to see that Wall, to see what it means and what the Chinese people have had in terms of a great history, but also what it means in terms of the future. That future is one toward which we are working, . . . a world in which no walls will divide people and divide nations, and in which they exist only for our protection and never for our division.

I would say finally that I was very moved by the poem the Prime Minister quoted and I would suggest that the poem had one omission. . . . Last night we saw women dance in the ballet, and the before we saw women athletes that were the equal of any man in the world. And there are those who communicate for the Prime Minister and me. We realize that true women should be honored as well as men.

So I raise my glass to the Prime Minister and all of our friends, but mainly to the true women.

DOCUMENT 6:

Senate Diet Hearings, 1973

Source: US Congress, Senate, Hearings before the Select Committee on Nutrition and Human Needs, Part 1, April 12, 1973.

During the disco era, calorie counting was becoming popular and major food producers cashed in by creating "lite" foods. Beers like Miller Lite claimed to "taste great" while being "less filling." Tab cola appealed to consumers who wanted to "keep tabs" on their calories. Diet gurus, like George Ohsawa and Robert Atkins, targeted their schemes to a fat and sugar conscious population. Ohsawa, a Japanese philosopher, promoted the macrobiotic diet, which centered vegetarian eating within a broad ecologically minded and spiritual worldview. Food historian Warren Belasco explained that with macrobiotics all matter was divided into yin and yang categories, and wholeness as well as health was attained "by reconciling these opposites." Atkins's diet, on the other hand, was more straightforward. Based on his interaction with patients as a practicing physician, Atkins urged dieters to cut down on carbohydrates for long-term weight reduction. However, the American Medical Association worried that the Atkins diet might be too high in fat and lacking in staples like grains, fruits, and dairy products for some people. Senator George McGovern, chair of the Senate Select Committee on Nutrition and Human Needs, was concerned about obesity and convened a series of hearings on fad diets to boost consumer knowledge.

Statement Announcing Hearing
by Senator George McGovern, Chairman

Next Thursday, April 12th, the Select Committee on Nutrition and Human Needs will hold the first in a series of hearings on nutrition and diseases with the problems of overweight and obesity in the United States. The hearing will explore two of the more popular diets in vogue today—macrobiotic diets, as proposed by the late Japanese philosopher Georges Ohsawa, and the "High Calorie Way to Stay Thin Forever" plan expounded by Robert C. Atkins, M.D. in his bestselling book *Dr. Atkins' Diet Revolution*. Both diets have been cited within the past 18 months by the American Medical Association's Council on Foods and Nutrition as nutritionally unsound and potentially dangerous.

Overweight, and its most acute form, obesity, afflict upwards of 30% of the American population. Associated with higher incidences of such major diseases as heart attacks and diabetes, overweight is found at all levels of the populace. No racial, sexual, age, ethnic or geographical group is free from overweight. Side-by-side with debilitating malnutrition, overweight, or "overnutrition," represents a tragic contradiction within modern American society. Some people get too little to eat; others eat too much. We have access to the most plentiful food supply system in the world, but due to a number of factors—bad dietary education and practice, the easy availability and poor quality of snack and junk foods, lack of exercise, and occasional physiological predispositions to overeating—prevalent overweight is generally a reflection of an affluent, sedentary lifestyle.

One of the more unfortunate results of widespread overweight is the so-called "diet industry." Chronically overweight individuals are the most vulnerable people in the marketplace, desperate to shed unhealthy and unwanted pounds. The rigors, bizarre cures and outright suffering these people subject themselves to is often compounded by the worthless, fraudulent nature of diet industry merchandise. Offering a blind array of health spas and clinics, miracle pills and powders, fad diets, exercise devices, reducing belts, saunas, togas, suits, and crèmes, the cost of [the] diet industry is estimated to be as high as $10 billion annually. The United States Postal Service, which monitors the mail order trade in diet products, advertised heavily in women's and pulp magazines, has stated that medical frauds are today more lucrative than another other criminal activity. . . .

By adhering to popularized diets without medical supervision, overweight people run the risk of not only further jeopardizing their already precarious health, but the health and nutrition of their children, including the unborn. Diet books are often instant bestsellers because of the ready market of overweight individuals, all eager to finally find the solution to their weight problem. Currently available diet plans run the gamut of the human imagination and vocabulary. Plans for the purchase at bookstores, health food shops, and through mail order firms suggest: the water diet, the rice diet, the milk and bananas diet, the grapefruit diet, the drinking man's diet, the lopsided egg diet, the starvation diet, the crash diet, the loving care diet, the macrobiotic diet, the eat all you want diet, the raw food diet, the organic fruit diet, the baked potato and buttermilk diet, the bread, cheese and wine diet, and so on, ad infinitum. The benefits offered run from instance weight loss, lifetime thinness and sexual prowess, to psychic awareness, philosophical bliss and cures for cancer, paralysis, schizophrenia and syphilis. And while the prescription drug and medical industries are under regulation by the Food and Drug Administration and other agencies, the diet industry, which produces potions and plans which often call for fundamental restructuring of an individual's dietary regimen, is virtually free from governmental restraints. The overweight consumer is the most unprotected consumer of all.

Over the past 18 months, the AMA has twice alerted its members and the public to the potential dangers of the diet recommendation of Mr. Georges Ohsawa and Dr. Robert Atkins. Atkins' book is, according to its publisher, David McKay Co., Inc., the fastest selling book in the history of publishing. Introduced in October 1972, the book has sold over 800,000 copies in hardbound at $6.95 each, and the 1 million mark is expected to be in print April 15th. Mr. Ohsawa's various macrobiotic books have been in circulation since 1965, and are in wide usage, owing primarily to the recent interest in natural foods, organic cooking, and the "back-to-the-earth movement," [and despite] particularly well-publicized, documented cases of severe injury and death associated with strict adherence to the diets, the Ohsawa books remain popular. A telephone survey March 29, 1973, of all health food stores listed in the Metropolitan Washington area Yellow Pages showed 66% of these stores (12 of 18) carried Ohsawa's diet books.

The continued easy availability of the Ohsawa books and the AMA's apparently inefficient warning raise questions about forming a suitable and effective method for informing the public about the potential health hazards presented by such popular diets.

CHAPTER 11

Contemporary Food Issues

By the late twentieth century, the issue of access to affordable, quality food had become a pressing political issue. The "standard American diet," which is high in fat and sugar and contains few fruits and vegetables, led to an epidemic of obesity. In 2012, 36 percent of Americans were overweight, and in 2013 the American Medical Association classified obesity as a "disease" in order to encourage more aggressive treatment of this potentially debilitating condition. There is a class component to this public health crisis because people living in poverty are more likely to be overweight than the affluent. The documents in this chapter highlight federal initiatives to encourage wholesome food practices and to provide food for the nation's neediest citizens. Critics of these government initiatives have argued that corporate lobbyists have encouraged the federal government to temper dietary recommendations that might hurt the financial interests of the producers of meat and processed foods.

Food reform advocate and author Michael Pollan, in his book *In Defense of Food: An Eater's Manifesto*, summarizes contemporary wisdom about proper eating habits with his advice: "Eat Food. Not too much. Mostly plants." Advice like this not only is designed to curb obesity but also is linked to a broader critique of the contemporary food system. A diverse group of activists known as the "Food Movement," with sometimes overlapping and sometimes distinct concerns, coalesced in the late twentieth century and remains active in the new millennium. Issues energizing these advocates range from pollution caused by pesticides and intensive meat-production facilities to cruelty to animals used as food, unequal access to healthy food, and beyond. Potential solutions to these problems have been posed by groups such as "locavores," who try to limit their environmental impact by eating wholesome food that has not been shipped long distances, and vegetarians and vegans who hope to limit pollution, improve human health, and end animal slaughter by removing meat or all animal products from the human diet. In document 6, James McWilliams offers a radical alternative to a key ingredient in the standard American diet, and in document 7, A. Breeze Harper urges food activists to be thoughtful about how issues of race and class impact ideas about healthful eating.

DOCUMENT 1:

Dietary Guidelines for Americans, 1980 and 1995

Source: US Department of Health and Human Services, Summary Chart of Guidelines, 1980–2000, health.gov.

Beginning in 1980, the US Department of Health and Human Services and the US Department of Agriculture have released a set of dietary guidelines for Americans every five years, offering advice based upon the latest nutritional research. These two sets of guidelines released in 1980 and 1995 show an evolution in the language used and also in the advice given. The most substantial change is the acknowledgment in the 1995 version that physical activity is an important component of a healthy lifestyle. This is likely a response to growing rates of obesity in the United States.

Dietary Guidelines 1980

Eat a variety of foods
Maintain ideal weight
Avoid too much fat, saturated fat, and cholesterol
Eat foods with adequate starch and fiber
Avoid too much sugar

Avoid too much sodium

If you drink alcohol, do so in moderation

Dietary Guidelines 1995

Eat a variety of foods

Balance the food you eat with physical activity—maintain or improve your weight

Choose a diet with plenty of grain products, vegetables, and fruits

Choose a diet low in fat, saturated fat, and cholesterol

Choose a diet moderate in sugars

Choose a diet moderate in salt and sodium

If you drink alcoholic beverages, do so in moderation

DOCUMENT 2:

The US Department of Agriculture Develops Educational Icons to Give Dietary Advice

Source: Foodpyramid.com and ChooseMyPlate. gov.

Document 2

In 1992 the US Department of Agriculture created the Food Guide Pyramid, an icon designed to visually capture the agency's healthful eating recommendation. In the 2005 version of the icon, each vertical stripe represents a food group and includes grains, vegetables, fruits, oil, milk, and meat and beans. The image includes a figure in motion to emphasize the idea that an exercise routine should accompany good eating habits. In 2010 the by then iconic pyramid was replaced with a dinner plate, which was designed to convey quickly the advice that half of a daily diet should consist of fruits and vegetables.

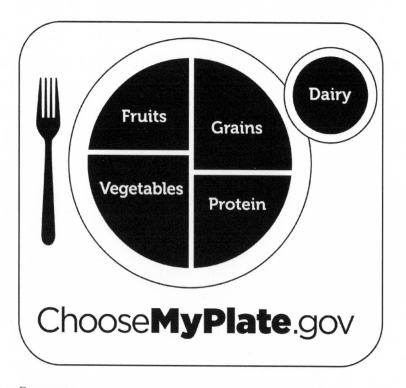

Document 2

CONTEMPORARY FOOD ISSUES

The US Department of Agriculture Certifies Some Food as Organic

Source: Ann H. Baier and Lisa Ahramjian,
"Organic Certification," www.ams.usda.gov

Concern over the harmful effects that pesticides have on the environment as well as upon human health has led an increasing number of consumers to demand access to fruits and vegetables grown using less toxic methods. In 1990 Congress passed the Organic Foods Production Act, which established guidelines for growers who wish to receive USDA certification that the food they produce meets new standards for "organic" produce. This 2012 document summarizes the criteria for USDA organic certification.

What is organic?

Organic is a labeling term for food or other agricultural products that have been produced according to the USDA organic regulations. These standards require the integration of cultural, biological, and mechanical practices that foster cycling of resources, promote ecological balance, and conserve biodiversity. This means that organic operations must maintain or enhance soil and water quality while also conserving wetlands, woodlands, and wildlife. Synthetic fertilizers, sewage sludge, irradiation, and genetic engineering may not be used.

All organic crops and livestock must be raised in a production system that emphasizes protection of natural resources; plant and animal health; preventative management of pests, diseases, and predators; and compliant use of allowed materials. All organic products must be protected from prohibited substances and methods from the field to the point of final sale, whether it is a raw agricultural commodity or a multi-ingredient, processed product. . . .

What is organic certification?

Organic certification verifies that your farm or handling facility located anywhere in the world complies with the U.S. Department of Agriculture (USDA) organic regulations and allows you to sell, label, and represent your products as organic. These regulations describe the specific standards required for you to use the word "organic" or the USDA organic seal on food, feed, or fiber products. The USDA National Organic Program (NOP) administers these regulations, with substantial input from its citizen advisory board and the public. . . .

Who needs to be certified?

If your farm or business receives *more than* $5,000 in gross annual organic sales, it must be certified.

If your farm or business receives *less than* $5,000 in gross annual organic sales, it is considered "exempt" from two key requirements.

Certification. Your farm or business doesn't need to be certified in order to sell, label, or represent your products as organic. However, you *may not* use the USDA organic seal on your products or refer to them as *certified* organic. If your operation is exempt and you would like to use the USDA organic seal, you are welcome to obtain optional organic certification. . . .

What types of products are eligible for organic certification?

USDA standards recognize four categories of organic production:

• Crops. Plants that are grown to be harvested as food, livestock feed, or fiber used to add nutrients to the field.

• Livestock. Animals that can be used for food or in the production of food, fiber, or feed.

• Processed/multi-ingredient products. Items that have been handled and packaged (e.g., chopped carrots) or combined, processed, and packaged (e.g., bread or soup).

• Wild crops. Plants from a growing site that is not cultivated.

Why is certification required?

In the 1980s, there were multiple organizations in the United States offering certification to different, and often conflicting, organic standards. Coupled with fraud and resulting consumer mistrust, this landscape created a need for Federal standards and oversight.

The Organic Foods Production Act of 1990 established national standards for the production and handling of organic agricultural products. The Act authorized USDA to create the NOP, which is responsible for developing, and ensuring compliance with, the USDA organic regulations.

Consumers choose to purchase organic products with the expectation that they are grown, processed, and handled according to the USDA organic regulations. A high-quality regulatory program benefits organic farmers and processors by taking action against those who violate the law and thereby jeopardize consumer confidence in organic products. . . .

What about other labeling claims?

All marketing claims, including organic, must reflect reality and fulfill truth-in-advertising rules. Many of these claims also require additional certification to government or association standards before they can be used. Examples of other claims that may or may not be appropriate for you to include on your organic product label include: Kosher, Halal, Fair Trade, biodynamic, free-range, grass-fed, humane, wildlife-friendly, and pesticide-free. Be sure that any and all terms are appropriately used.

DOCUMENT 4:

The Federal Government Justifies Providing Subsistence for the Nation's Poorest Citizens

Source: United States Department of Agriculture, "Building a Healthy America," fns. usda.gov

In the twenty-first century, economic inequality is dramatically manifested in the realm of food culture. While wealthy Americans are able to see food as a form of entertainment and spend hundreds of dollars on elaborate

meals at restaurants presided over by celebrity chefs, other Americans go hungry. According to US Department of Agriculture statistics, in 2010, 14.5 percent of households in the United States were food insecure, and 5.4 percent had very low food security. For some, food insecurity is characterized by having access to a limited variety of unhealthful foods. For others, it can mean actual physical hunger. The poorest Americans have access to the Supplemental Nutrition Assistance Program (SNAP), which provides government monies to buy food. And 47 million individuals, or one in seven Americans, relied on SNAP in 2014. For those receiving assistance, benefits average out at $133.85 per individual each month. Despite the meager level of subsistence provided by this government program, many politicians have decried its existence, stigmatizing the recipients of the program as undeserving and lazy. In this document the US Department of Agriculture defends SNAP.

Building a Healthy America:
A Profile of the Supplemental Nutrition Assistance Program United States Department of Agriculture

For more than 40 years, the Supplemental Nutrition Assistance Program (SNAP) has served as the foundation of America's national nutrition safety net. It is the nation's first line of defense against hunger and offers a powerful tool to improve nutrition among low-income people. In fiscal year 2011, SNAP served nearly 45 million people, about one in seven Americans.

Over the course of four decades, researchers and analysts—inside government and out—have built a substantial body of evidence that SNAP makes an important difference in the lives of low-income people.

- It touches the lives of millions of people who need help to put food on the table. Unlike most other assistance programs, SNAP is available to nearly anyone who qualifies with little income and few resources. Program rules do not limit benefits to families with children or the elderly or the unemployed. Nationwide standards for eligibility and benefits create a national nutrition safety net for low-income families and individuals wherever they live.

- It supports those whose wages are too low to lift them out of poverty. SNAP is an important work support: 75 percent of the people who receive benefits for a year or less—and about 40 percent overall—live in households with earnings. The Census Bureau indicates that SNAP would lift 3.9 million Americans— including 1.7 million children—out of poverty in 2010 if its benefits were included in the official measures of income and poverty.

- It raises food expenditures and improves nutrient availability. Participants in SNAP spend more on food than they would in the absence of the program. Providing benefits that can be spent only on food raises food expenditures more than an equal amount of cash. In addition, there is evidence that program participation can increase the availability of some nutrients in the home food supply. Recent studies have shown that the nutrient intake of low-income people differs little from higher-income people—a sharp contrast from 40 years ago.

- It responds to changing economic conditions. The program automatically expands to meet increased need when the economy is in recession and contracts when the economy is growing, making sure that food gets to people who need it. SNAP benefits automatically flow to communities, States, or regions of the country that face rising unemployment or poverty, providing a boost for local economies. When the economy strengthens, SNAP participation declines.

- It delivers benefits with a high degree of integrity. The program effectively delivers benefits only to households that need them: more than 98 percent of all participating households are eligible for SNAP benefits. In fiscal year 2010, the program achieved the highest level of overall payment accuracy in its history: the national overpayment error rate—the percentage of SNAP benefit dollars issued in excess of the amounts for which households are eligible—fell to 3.05 percent; the underpayment error rate was less than 1.00 percent. Trafficking is the sale of SNAP benefits for cash, a practice that diverts benefits away from their intended purpose of helping low-income families access a nutritious diet. The extent of trafficking is also low, about one cent of every dollar issued.

- It provides flexibility to States while ensuring the protection of a national safety net. The Food, Conservation, and Energy Act of 2008 (2008 Farm Bill) continued the commitment to a national nutrition safety net and gave States a substantial new opportunity to streamline complex rules. In addition, States may also use SNAP's waiver procedures to test changes to a variety of program rules. . . .

How SNAP Works

SNAP alleviates hunger and improves nutrition by increasing the food purchasing power of low-income households, enabling them to obtain a more nutritious diet by preparing food at home.

The program is available to nearly anyone with little income and few resources who qualifies. Program rules do not limit benefits to a specific group of people, such as the elderly, families with children, or the unemployed. As a result, the program serves a wide range of low-income persons, about half of whom are children.

Nationwide standards for eligibility and benefits create a national safety net for low-income households. Generally SNAP households must have monthly gross income less than 130 percent of the Federal poverty guidelines ($2,422 for a family of four in fiscal year 2012), monthly net income less than 100 percent of the poverty guidelines, and assets of less than $2,000. Households with elderly (age 60 and older) and disabled members are exempt from the gross income limit and must have assets less than $3,250. Categorical eligibility exempts households from the income and asset tests if all members receive Temporary Assistance for Needy Families (TANF), State General Assistance, or Supplemental Security Income (SSI). Broad-based categorical eligibility (BBCE), a State option, may extend the exemption from the asset and income tests to additional families receiving a TANF-funded benefit or service. Eligible households must also meet some nonfinancial criteria, including citizenship and work requirements. Almost all households that reside in States with BBCE would be eligible for SNAP under standard program rules.

National standards for application filing and processing also bolster the safety net. SNAP has standard procedures for application filing, interviews, verification of applicant information, and application processing that provide strong procedural protections for applicants and participants.

The program allows several deductions from income, to provide a better measure of disposable income available to purchase food and to encourage work. The deductions include a standard available to all households; an earned income deduction available to working households; a shelter deduction for those with high shelter expenses; and dependent care, medical, and child support deductions for some with particular expenses. These deductions are subtracted from gross income to determine net income.

SNAP benefits are based on the Thrifty Food Plan, a minimal cost food plan that reflects current nutrition standards and guidance, the nutrient content and cost of food, and consumption patterns of low-income households. Maximum allotments vary by household size. In fiscal year 2012, the maximum allotment for a family of four is $668 per month, including the benefit increase contained in The American Recovery and Reinvestment Act of 2009 (Recovery Act).

Maximum allotments are reduced by 30 percent of a household's net income. SNAP benefits are designed to be a supplement to food purchases made with the household's own income. As a result, benefits can vary across households of the same gross income and size.

Participating households receive monthly benefit allotments in the form of electronic debit cards (also known as EBT, or electronic benefit transfer). SNAP benefits are limited to the purchase of food items for use at home as well as seeds and plants to produce food. Alcohol and tobacco cannot be purchased with SNAP benefits. Many States use a single EBT card for SNAP and a variety of cash benefit programs. The cash benefits can be accessed through most ATMs, but SNAP benefits cannot be withdrawn as cash.

SNAP benefits are used at supermarkets, large and small grocery stores, convenience and specialty stores, and farmers markets. Benefits can be exchanged only at authorized food retailers. Nationwide, there were about 230,000 authorized retailers at the end of fiscal year 2011.

Benefits are 100 percent Federally funded, whereas administrative costs are shared between States and the Federal government. Although broad policy guidance is provided through USDA's Food and Nutrition Service (FNS), day-to-day administration is carried out by States or counties. States are responsible for the certification of households and issuance of benefits. FNS is responsible for the authorization and oversight of food retailers.

The program monitors performance through a national system of quality control and a set of participation indicators. The quality control system measures the accuracy of eligibility decisions and benefit determinations against program rules for a representative sample of cases. Other performance measures include the proportion of eligible households who receive benefits and the percentage of applications processed within required timelines. . . .

Why SNAP Is Important

SNAP participation grows when the economy is weak, helping families put food on the table. As the number of unemployed persons and families living in poverty grew in the last few years, so did SNAP participation. When the economy improves, SNAP participation will decline. The face of SNAP has changed during the recent economic downturn as more newly unemployed or underemployed people rely on SNAP to feed their families. Although SNAP largely serves a vulnerable population—children, elderly, and individuals with disabilities—it is available to most individuals with low incomes who meet the eligibility criteria. At the end of fiscal year 2011, SNAP was serving about one in seven Americans.

SNAP helps prevent food insecurity. The number of households experiencing food insecurity, or difficulty getting enough food because of a lack of resources, was at record high levels in 2008 to 2010. Although the continued high levels of food insecurity are cause for concern, the fact that the numbers did not increase between 2008 and 2010, despite a significant increase in the poverty rate and number of unemployed persons, underscores the important role of SNAP in helping to prevent food insecurity.

SNAP lifts millions of people out of poverty. The Census Bureau has reported that 46.2 million people—15.1 percent of all those in the United States—lived in poverty in 2010. SNAP benefits have a powerful anti-poverty effect that is not reflected in the Nation's official poverty statistics. The Census Bureau indicates that SNAP would lift 3.9 million Americans—including 1.7 million children—out of poverty if its benefits were included in the official measures of income and poverty. Another study found that the antipoverty effectiveness of SNAP accelerated over the decade, with about 2 million people lifted out of poverty each year through 2003, but that figure more than doubled to 4.5 million in 2009 because of the deep recession and the benefit increase in the Recovery Act.

SNAP provides a fiscal boost to the economy during an economic downturn. In addition to helping families during these tough economic times, SNAP has an added benefit of serving as an economic multiplier—meaning it puts critical dollars back into local economies. Every $1 in new benefits generates up to $1.80 in economic activity. Every time a family uses SNAP benefits to put healthy food on the table, it benefits the store and the employees where the purchase was made, the truck driver who delivered the food, the warehouses that stored it, the plant that processed it, and the farmer who produced the food. Each $1 billion increase in SNAP benefits is estimated to create or maintain 18,000 full-time equivalent jobs, including 3,000 farm jobs.

DOCUMENT 5:

Let's Move! Factsheet

Source: letsmove.gov

First Lady Michelle Obama has been an ardent healthful food advocate since her husband was first elected in 2008. From initiating a White House garden to promoting exercise and careful food choices, she has helped sustain a national dialogue on curbing obesity. Though there has been some negative reaction to her advocacy, she has made information about nutrition and healthy living more widely available to working-class Americans who lack the financial and institutional resources of the middle class. She has, for example, worked to convince discount grocery stores like Walmart that selling healthier foods can be profitable. In 2010 she founded Let's Move!, an initiative that focuses on fighting childhood obesity.

The Facts

Let's Move! is a comprehensive initiative, launched by the First Lady, dedicated to solving the problem of childhood obesity in a generation so that kids born today will grow up healthier and able to pursue their dreams. This is an ambitious goal. But it can be done.

Combining comprehensive strategies with common sense, Let's Move! is about putting children on the path to a healthy future starting with their earliest months and years and continuing throughout their lives. Giving parents helpful information and fostering environments that support healthy choices. Providing healthier foods in our schools. Ensuring that every community has access to healthy, affordable food. And, helping kids become more physically active.

The Issue

Over the past three decades, childhood obesity rates in America have tripled. Today, almost one in every three children in our nation is overweight or obese. The numbers are even higher in African American and Hispanic communities where nearly 40% of the children are overweight or obese. Rates are estimated to be even higher in American Indian/Alaska Native communities. If we don't solve this problem, one third of all children born in 2000 or later will suffer from diabetes at some point in their lives. Many others will face chronic obesity-related health problems like heart disease, high blood pressure, cancer and asthma.

The Solution

Encourage kids to eat healthier and move more. When children combine physical activity with healthy eating in their daily routine, they help prevent a range of chronic diseases, including heart disease, cancer and stroke—the three leading causes of death. Along with decreasing obesity risk, physical activity helps to control weight, build lean muscle, reduce fat and promote strong bone, muscle and joint development. Physical activity has also been shown to improve academic performance including better grades, test scores, classroom behavior, attention, and concentration. And, of course, healthy eating gives kids the proper nutrition they need to stay energized, active, and maintain a healthy weight.

Let's Get Moving

Get kids moving and make healthier choices for your children.

- Children need 60 minutes of active and vigorous play each day.
- Serve fruit or veggies with every meal.
- Substitute water or low-fat milk for sweetened beverages.
- Pick a vegetable they like and find different, tasty ways to prepare it.
- Substitute healthier ingredients such as whole wheat pasta and lean meats in their favorite recipes.
- Eat meals as a family.

DOCUMENT 6:

James McWilliams Advocates for Meatless Hot Dogs

Source: "No Dog Hot Dog Good Dog," July 3, 2012, jamesmcwilliams.com.

Concern for animal welfare and environmental degradation associated with intensive meat production has led a growing number of Americans to limit their consumption of animal products. In the twenty-first century, about 10 percent of the US population can be characterized as "flexitarians" who endeavor to eat meat sparingly. More than seven million Americans are vegetarians who consume dairy and eggs but not animal flesh. One million are vegans who will not consume any animal products. In this posting from his blog Eating Plants, *historian James McWilliams proposes a vegan alternative to the iconic American hot dog.*

No Dog Hot Dog Good Dog

Why anybody would eat a traditional hot dog, behavioral omnivores included, is beyond me. It's long been known that most hot dogs are rendered from slaughterhouse refuse that makes pink slime look like health food. "Everything but the squeal" is a phrase that has served to capture this reality with pithy, if tasteless, humor. More pointedly, the claim that a hot dog is comprised of little more than "lips and assholes," a vivid description many of us first heard as children, remains rather hard to shake. Even when I ate meat I was enlightened enough to avoid these disgusting cylinders of junk like the plague. In a word, *nasty*.

Leave it to Americans to glorify this waste receptacle as "all-American" food—food that must roll off a grill and adulterate the patriotic palate of every red-blooded American on the 4th of July. Not only that, but leave it to Americans, as our culinary reputation improves, to dress the dog up into something fancier than it really is, hiding its humble identity in clothing purloined from alien emperors.

Indeed, as you have *no doubt* heard: a hot dog renaissance is underway in the U. S. of A, with top chefs and foodie savants gussying up this bun-full of cruelty into a gourmet creation, selling their wares from food cart windows in hip cities across the landscape. If there's any hope in this admittedly dubious transition it's this: hot dog entrepreneurs are hiding the dog under heaps of delicious fruits and vegetables.

Yes indeed, the standard toppings—mustard, ketchup, raw onions, and relish—is slowly yielding to a more sophisticated array of tomatoes, peppers, mangoes, pineapple, kimchee, cucumbers, caramelized onions and sesame seeds. Needless to say, the standard fare is also being adulterated with bacon, cream cheese, and turkey. But still, if my brief survey of the changes underway are at all accurate, my sense is that the good stuff is being piled higher than the bad stuff. A mild improvement on the average, I'd say.

But, you are thinking, so what? . . . Well, here's so what: what if the dog quietly slipped out the back, leaving behind a mound of plant matter to enjoy?

I realize that a hot-dog-less hot dog sounds quirky, but do consider: The worst and best quality about "American food" is that it's endlessly adaptable. Americans have no culinary allegiance; our tradition is to have no tradition. The United States may be the only place where the prospect of a hot-dog-less hot dog could become a reality, however remote the possibility. (It may also—a topic for another post—be the most likely place to embrace veganism as a mass movement.)

Several readers of my recent "fake meat" blog post astutely noted that what lends flavor to animal products are in fact plant-based products, thus persuading me that my analysis was not as convincing as I'd initially thought. It might seem desperate for me to seek hope in a hot dog without the hot dog, but it is in the spirit of plant-based-flavor-power that I ask you to imagine the future of the "hot dog" being a whole grain bun piled with a creative array of fruits, veggies, herbs, spices, and nuts. Dare to dream.

The hot dog could be the American version of the banh mi sandwich, open to vegan interpretation, conducive to regional styles, and—most importantly—a hell of a lot more patriotic that slaughtering hundreds of millions of pigs and cows, gathering the offal, making a gross tube of it, and calling it, however inexplicably, a dog.

DOCUMENT 7:

A. Breeze Harper Urges the Food Movement to Be Sensitive to Issues of Race and Class

Source: "Revisiting Racialized Consciousness
and Black Female Vegan Experiences: An
Interview," December 6, 2009, sistahvegan.com

In this posting from her blog Sistah Vegan, *food studies scholar A. Breeze Harper offers a critique of activists in the Food Movement who are insensitive to what she sees as the racial and class implications of their specific style of activism.*

I have observed that alternative food movements are not necessarily inclusive of food justice activism. Things such as Farmer's Markets, CSAs, and Slow Food are alternative but its constituency are largely white class privileged people who really aren't reflecting on white privilege and how structural racism have made it a great challenge for non-white racialized people and the working poor to have access to nutritious foods. . . . Veganism for a significant number of practitioners is an alternative food praxis, but I would argue that many do not engage in food justice veganism that is critically reflective of white racial privilege as well as US American privilege.

Practitioners of veganism abstain from animal consumption and a majority support animal rights. However, the culture of veganism itself is not a monolith and is in fact comprised of many different subcultures and philosophies throughout the world, ranging from punk strict vegans for animal rights, to people who are dietary vegans for personal health reasons, to people who practice veganism for religious and spiritual reasons. The Vegan Society, the organization that coined the term "vegan," states that the heart of veganism calls for practice of Ahimsa or "compassion, kindness, and justice" for all living beings. However it must be understood that veganism, at least in the United States of America, has the connotation of being a lifestyle of white socio-economic class privileged people. Indeed on the popular satirical online site, *Stuff White People Like*, creator Christian Lander jokingly writes, "As with many white people activities, being vegan/vegetarian enables them to feel as though they are helping the environment AND it gives them a sweet way to feel superior to others." Lander's humor plays on exposing the overwhelming whiteness of the vegan/animal rights movement.

Other vegan texts ignore issues of race and class completely. For example, considered part of the vegan mainstream, the *New York Times* bestselling vegan book series *Skinny Bitch*, promote veganism as a way for women to lose weight, be healthy, and alleviate suffering of non-human animals. If one considers looking at the vegan pregnancy title, *Skinny Bitch: Bun in the Oven* through a critical race and black feminist analytical lens, the tone of book reveals that the book's assumed audience is white middle-class heterosexual females who live in locations where a whole foods vegan diet is easily accessible (geographically and financially). At the beginning of each new chapter of the book, there is always a depiction of a white skinny pregnant woman. Throughout the text, the authors blame personal laziness as the reason why people are overweight. This top selling title is an example of a "race doesn't matter" (and class doesn't either) approach to vegan living as well as food justice. There is never any reflection on how: (1) class and the racialized experience in the USA affect a pregnant woman's access to healthful food and nutritional information; and (2) how the author's white racialized and class privileged consciousness influence their perception of veganism as the easy "no brainer" answer to obesity problems. Though the author's intent of the book was not to focus on racialized and classed experiences of veganism and pregnancy, the absence of this personal reflection and assumptions made about their audience, amongst these authors (who are white and class privileged), are intriguing and quite telling.

Texts such as the *Skinny Bitch* series engage in a "lack of color/race conscious" approach to food politics that ignores the effects of race and class on an individual's circumstances and the range of options available to her. In a "post-racial" or "raceless" society, it is believed that racism no longer exists because skin color no longer has social significance. For example, if a white person were to tell their Chinese friend, "I don't think of you as Chinese, I am colorblind," I argue that this Chinese friend would not be seen as race-neutral, but in fact seen by their friend as, "I don't think of you as Chinese, I just think of you as if you were any other [white] person." The phenomenon I'm analyzing is actually part of a larger body of scholarly work around the issues of whiteness and white privilege. . . .

My research activism focuses on the under-researched topic of intersections of vegan philosophy and race/racism/racialized consciousness. My creation of *Sistah Vegan* came out of my desire to create a black female socio-spatial epistemological stance around veganism, simply because no one had ever done it before. When I would visit mainstream vegan forums, several years ago, veganism was only oriented toward animal rights as priority. However, a significant number of black female identified vegans that I had dialogued with had come to veganism from a completely different angle: reclaiming their womb health and fighting black health disparities. It was a clear indicator to me that the way one comes to, and engages in, veganism is heavily influenced by racialized and gendered experiences.

FOR FURTHER READING

Abarca, Meredith E. *Voices in the Kitchen: Views of Food and the World from Working-Class Mexican and Mexican American Women*. College Station: Texas A&M Press, 2006.

Anderson, Oscar Edward. *Refrigeration in America: A History of a New Technology and Its Impact*. Princeton, NJ: Princeton University Press, 1953.

Belasco, Warren. *Appetite for Change: How the Counterculture Took on the Food Industry*. Ithaca, NY: Cornell University Press, 2006.

———. *Food: The Key Concepts*. Oxford: Berg, 2008.

Bentley, Amy. *Eating for Victory: Food Rationing and the Politics of Domesticity*. Chicago: University of Illinois Press, 1998.

Berzok, Linda Murray. *American Indian Food*. Westport, CT: Greenwood Press, 2005.

Bienvenu, Marcelle, Carl A. Brasseaux, and Ryan A. Brasseaux. *Stir the Pot: The History of Cajun Cuisine*. New York: Hippocrene Books, 2005.

Biltekoff, Charlotte. *Eating Right in America: The Cultural Politics of Food and Health*. Durham: Duke University Press, 2013.

Bower, Ann L., ed. *African American Foodways: Explorations of History and Culture*. Urbana: University of Illinois, 2007.

Brenner, Leslie. *American Appetite: The Coming of Age of a National Cuisine*. New York: Perennial, 1997.

Brown, Linda Keller, and Kay Mussell. *Ethnic and Regional Foodways in the United States: The Performance of Group Identity*. Knoxville: University of Tennessee Press, 1984.

Carney, Judith. *Black Rice: The African Origins of Rice Cultivation in the Americas*. Cambridge: Harvard University Press, 2001.

Carney, Judith A., and Richard Nicholas Rosomoff. *In the Shadow of Slavery: Africa's Botanical Legacy in the Atlantic World*. Berkeley: University of California Press, 2009.

Coe, Andrew. *Chop Suey: A Cultural History of Chinese Food in the United States*. Oxford: Oxford University Press, 2009.

Collingham, Lizzie. *The Taste of War: World War II and the Battle for Food*. New York: Penguin Books, 2013.

Covey, Herbert C., and Dwight Eisnach. *What the Slaves Ate: Recollections of African American Foods and Foodways from Slave Narratives*. Santa Barbara, CA: ABC-CLIO, 2009.

Cowan, Ruth Schwartz. *More Work for Mother: The Ironies of Household Technology from the Open Hearth to the Microwave*. New York: Basic Books, 1983.

Curtin, Kathleen, and Sandra L. Oliver. *Giving Thanks: Thanksgiving Recipes and History, from Pilgrims to Pumpkin Pie*. New York: Clarkson Potter, 2005.

Davidson, Alan. *The Oxford Companion to Food*. Oxford: Oxford University Press, 2006.

DeWitt, Dave. *The Founding Foodies: How Washington, Jefferson, and Franklin Revolutionized American Cuisine*. Naperville, IL: Sourcebooks, 2010.

Diner, Hasia R. *Hungering for America: Italian, Irish, and Jewish Foodways in the Age of Migration*. Cambridge, MA: Harvard University Press, 2001.

Eden, Trudy. *The Early American Table: Food and Society in the New World*. Dekalb: Northern Illinois University Press, 2008.

Edge, John T., ed. *The New Encyclopedia of Southern Culture: Foodways*. Chapel Hill: University of North Carolina Press, 2007.

Elias, Megan J. *Food in the United States, 1890–1945*. Santa Barbara, CA: ABC-CLIO, 2009.

———. *Stir It Up: Home Economics in American Culture*. Philadelphia: University of Pennsylvania Press, 2008.

Engelhardt, Elizabeth. *A Mess of Greens: Southern Gender and Southern Food*. Athens: University of Georgia Press, 2011.

Fernández-Armesto, Felipe. *Near a Thousand Tables: A History of Food*. New York: Free Press, 2002.

Foer, Jonathon Safran. *Eating Animals*. New York: Little, Brown and Company, 2009.

Gabaccia, Donna R. *We Are What We Eat: Ethnic Food and the Making of Americans*. Cambridge, MA: Harvard University Press, 1998.

Haber, Barbara. *From Hardtack to Home Fries: An Uncommon History of American Cooks and Meals*. New York: Penguin Books, 2002.

Hailman, John. *Thomas Jefferson on Wine*. Jackson: University Press of Mississippi, 2006.

Haley, Andrew P. *Turning the Tables: Restaurants and the Rise of the American Middle Class, 1880–1920*. Chapel Hill: University of North Carolina Press, 2011.

Hardeman, Nicholas P. *Shucks, Shocks, and Hominy Blocks: Corn as a Way of Life in Pioneer America*. Baton Rouge: Louisiana State University Press, 1981.

Harris, Jessica B. *High on the Hog: A Culinary Journey from Africa to America*. New York: Bloomsbury, 2011.

Hauck-Lawson, Annie, and Jonathon Deutsch, eds. *Gastropolis: Food and New York City*. New York: Columbia University Press, 2009.

Hess, John L., and Karen Hess. *The Taste of America*. Champaign: University of Illinois Press, 2000.

Hess, Karen. *The Carolina Rice Kitchen: The African Connection*. Columbia: University of South Carolina Press, 1992.

Hilliard, Sam Bowers. *Hog Meat and Hoecake: Food Supply in the Old South, 1840–1860*. Carbondale: University of Illinois Press, 1972.

Horowitz, Roger. *Putting Meat on the American Table*. Baltimore: Johns Hopkins University Press, 2006.

Horsman, Reginald. *Feast or Famine: Food and Drink in American Westward Expansion*. Columbia: University of Missouri Press, 2008.

Inness, Sherrie A., ed. *Kitchen Culture in America: Popular Representatives of Food, Gender, and Race*. Philadelphia: University of Pennsylvania Press, 2001.

———. *Secret Ingredients: Race, Gender, and Class at the Dinner Table*. New York: Palgrave Macmillan, 2006.

Janer, Zilkia. *Latino Food Culture*. Westport, CT: Greenwood, 2008.

Kamps, Alice D. *What's Cooking, Uncle Sam? The Government's Effect on the American Diet*. Washington, DC: The Foundation for the National Archives, 2011.

LaCombe, Michael. *Political Gastronomy: Food and Authority in the English Atlantic World*. Philadelphia: University of Pennsylvania Press, 2012.

Levenstein, Harvey. *Fear of Food: A History of Why We Worry about What We Eat*. Chicago: University of Chicago Press, 2012.

———. *Paradox of Plenty: A Social History of Eating in Modern America*. New York: Oxford University Press, 1993.

―――. *Revolution at the Table: The Transformation of the American Diet.* Berkeley: University of California Press, 2003.

Long, Lucy M., ed. *Culinary Tourism.* Lexington: University of Kentucky Press, 2004.

Madden, Etta M., and Martha L. Finch, eds. *Eating in Eden: Food and American Utopias.* Lincoln: University of Nebraska Press, 2006.

Mariani, John. *America Eats Out: An Illustrated History of Restaurants, Taverns, Coffee Shops, Speakeasies, and Other Establishments that Have Fed Us for 350 Years.* New York: William Morrow, 1991.

―――. *The Dictionary of American Food and Drink.* New Haven: Ticknor and Fields, 1983.

McFeely, Mary Drake. *Can She Bake a Cherry Pie: American Women and the Kitchen in the Twentieth Century.* Amherst: University of Massachusetts Press, 2000.

McWilliams, James. *Just Food: Where Locavores Get It Wrong and How We Can Truly Eat Responsibly.* New York: Little, Brown & Company, 2009.

―――. *A Revolution in Eating: How the Quest for Food Shaped America.* New York: Columbia University Press, 2005.

Meacham, Sarah Hand. *Every Home a Distillery: Alcohol, Gender, and Technology in the Colonial Chesapeake.* Baltimore: Johns Hopkins University, 2009.

Miller, Adrian. *Soul Food: The Surprising Story of an American Cuisine One Plate at a Time.* Chapel Hill: University of North Carolina Press, 2013.

Miller, Jeff, and Jonathan Deutsch. *Food Studies: An Introduction to Research Methods.* Oxford: Berg, 2009.

Nestle, Marion. *Food Politics: How the Food Industry Influences Nutrition and Health.* Berkeley: University of California Press, 2002.

Nissenbaum, Stephen. *Sex, Diet, and Debility in Jacksonian America: Sylvester Graham and Health Reform.* Westport, CT: Greenwood Press, 1980.

Oliver, Sandra L. *Food in Colonial and Federal America.* Westport, CT: Greenwood Press, 2005.

―――. *Saltwater Foodways: New Englanders and Their Food at Sea and Ashore in the Nineteenth Century.* Mystic, CT: Mystic Seaport Museum, 1970.

Opie, Frederick Douglass. *Hog and Hominy: Soul Food from Africa to America.* New York: Columbia University Press, 2008.

Pilcher, Jeffrey M. *Food in World History*. New York: Routledge, 2006.

———, ed. *The Oxford Handbook of Food History*. Oxford: Oxford University Press, 2012.

———. *Planet Taco: A Global History of Mexican Food*. Oxford: Oxford University Press, 2012.

———. *¡Que vivan los tamales! Food and the Making of Mexican Identity*. Albuquerque: University of New Mexico Press, 1998.

Pillsbury, Richard. *No Foreign Food: The American Diet in Time and Place*. Boulder, CO: Westview Press, 1998.

Pollan, Michael. *Cooked: A Natural History of Transformation*. New York: Penguin Books, 2013.

———. *In Defense of Food: An Eater's Manifesto*. New York: Penguin Books, 2008.

———. *The Omnivore's Dilemma: A Natural History of Four Meals*. New York: Penguin, 2006.

Root, Waverly, and Richard de Rochement. *Eating in America: A History*. New York: William & Morrow, 1976.

Schenone, Laura. *A Thousand Years over a Hot Stove*. New York: W. W. Norton, 2003.

Shapiro, Laura. *Perfection Salad: Women and Cooking at the Turn of the Twentieth Century*. Berkeley: University of California Press, 1986.

———. *Something from the Oven: Reinventing Dinner in 1950s America*. New York: Viking, 2004.

Sharpless, Rebecca. *Cooking in Other Women's Kitchens*. Chapel Hill: University of North Carolina Press, 2010.

Shepard, Sue. *Pickled, Potted, and Canned: How the Art and Science of Food Preserving Changed the World*. New York: Simon & Schuster, 2000.

Shortridge, Barbara G., and James R. Shortridge, eds. *The Taste of American Place: A Reader on Regional and Ethnic Foods*. Lanham, MD: Rowman & Littlefield, 1998.

Shprintzen, Adam D. *The Vegetarian Crusade: The Rise of an American Reform Movement, 1817–1921*. Chapel Hill: University of North Carolina Press, 2013.

Siegel, Don. *From Lokshen to Lo Mein: The Jewish Affair with Chinese Food*. Jerusalem: Gefen Publishing, 2005.

Singer, Peter, and Jim Mason. *The Ethics of What We Eat: Why Our Food Choices Matter*. Emmaus, PA: Rodale Books, 2006.

Smith, Andrew F. *Eating History: 30 Turning Points in the Making of American Cuisine*. New York: Columbia University Press, 2009.

———. *The Oxford Companion to American Food and Drink*. Oxford: Oxford University Press, 2007.

Sokolow, Jayme A. *Eros and Modernization: Sylvester Graham, Health Reform, and the Origins of Victorian Sexuality in America*. Rutherford: Fairleigh Dickinson Press, 1983.

Stavely, Keith, and Kathleen Fitzgerald. *America's Founding Food: The Story of New England Cooking*. Chapel Hill: University of North Carolina Press, 2004.

Strasser, Susan. *Never Done: A History of American Housework*. New York: Henry Holt and Company, 2000.

Tannahill, Reay. *Food in History*. New York: Three Rivers Press, 1988.

Taylor, Joe Gray. *Eating, Drinking, and Visiting in the South: An Informal History*. Baton Rouge: Louisiana State University Press, 1982.

Theopano, Janet. *Eat My Words: Reading Women's Lives through the Cookbooks They Wrote*. New York: Palgrave, 2002.

Veit, Helen Zoe. *Modern Food, Moral Food: Self-Control, Science, and the Rise of Modern American Eating in the Early Twentieth Century*. Chapel Hill: University of North Carolina Press, 2013.

Wallach, Jennifer Jensen. *How America Eats: A Social History of US Food and Culture*. Lanham, MD: Rowman and Littlefield, 2013.

Weatherwax, Paul. *Indian Corn in Old America*. New York: Macmillan Company, 1954.

Williams, Jacqueline. *Wagon Wheels Kitchens: Food on the Oregon Trail*. Lawrence: University Press of Kansas, 1993.

Williams, Susan. *Food in the United States: 1820s–1890*. Westport, CT: Greenwood Press, 2006.

———. *Savory Suppers and Fashionable Feasts: Dining in Victorian America*. New York: Pantheon, 1985.

Williams-Forson, Psyche. *Building Houses out of Chicken Legs: Black Women, Food, and Power*. Chapel Hill: University of North Carolina Press, 2006.

Wilson, David Scofield, and Angus Kress Gillespie, eds. *Rooted in America: Foodlore of Popular Fruits and Vegetables*. Knoxville: University of Tennessee Press, 1999.

Wright, Clarissa Dickson. *A History of English Food*. New York: Random House, 2011.

Ziegelman, Jane. *97 Orchard: An Edible History of Five Immigrant Families in One New York Tenement*. New York: Harper Collins, 2010.

INDEX

Abel, Mary Hinman, 136–40
abolitionists, 79
acorns, 38
Adams, John, 49
adolescent girls, xxi, 124–25
adulterated food, 123
Africa. *See* West Africa
African Americans: civil rights
    movement, 187, 188–91; foodway
    histories, 148–51; Great Migration,
    148–49; tenant farming, 147;
    veganism, 223–25
Agricultural Adjustment Act (1933),
    147, 156
agricultural practices: Louisiana, 12–19;
    Timucua Indians, 20–22; West
    Africa, 26–31
Alabama, 79
alcohol consumption effects, 155
alcoholic beverages, 27
alcoholism, 133
alcohol prohibition, 147, 151–54
Algonquin, 31–32, 37–38
American Cookery (Simmons), 50–51
American Frugal Housewife, The
    (Child), 62–65
Americanization through Homemaking
    (Ellis), 133
American Medical Association (AMA),
    204, 206, 207
American Recovery and Reinvestment
    Act (2009), 217
Amerindian food habits: Arapaho, 4–5;
    background information, 3–4;
    Carlisle Indian Industrial School,
    124, 135–36; colonial period, 31–38;
    Iroquois, 6–8; mestizo cuisine,
    61–62; Pueblo Indians, 8–9, 61,
    72–73; subsistence strategies,
    20–22; Timucua Indians, 20–22;
    Wichita Indians, 9–11

animal processing. *See* unsanitary
    meat-processing facilities
animal rights movement, 223–25.
    See also veganism
Anti-Saloon League, 151, 154–55
Apalachean beans, 15
appliances, innovative, 166, 180–81,
    184–85
Arapaho, 4–5
Arkansas State Capitol, 187, 188–91
artichokes, 38
assimilation: ethnic minorities, 132–35;
    immigrant populations, 123;
    Native Americans, 123–24, 135–36
Atkins, Robert, 204, 206

baby formulae kitchen, 173
bacon, 173
bananas, 173
barbed wire, 70
barley, 14, 24
basic food groups, 177–79
Battle Creek Sanitarium health facility,
    124
beans: colonial period, 31; food groups,
    142; good cooking skills, 131;
    Iroquois, 6–8; Louisiana, 14–15;
    meat substitutes, 143; nutritional
    recommendations, 178, 179;
    Pueblo Indians, 9; tenant farming,
    157; West African diet, 27; Wichita
    Indians, 10
bears, 9, 10, 38
beaver, 38
Beecher, Catherine E., 129–32
beef, 39–40, 64, 115, 121, 173, 179
beer, 14
beets, 173
Belasco, Warren, 204
Benin, 26
bills of fare, 137–40

honey, 27, 143
Hoover, Herbert, 141, 147
horse-beans, 29
horses, 5, 38
hot dogs, 167, 171–72, 173, 221–23
Hotpoint, 180
housekeeping advice, 62–65, 80–83, 98–100
housewife/homemaker training: Beecher and Stowe, 129–32; economically disadvantaged populations, 136–40; Native Americans, 135–36
Houston, Texas, 162–63
How to Be Plump, Or Talks on Physiological Feeding (Duncan), xxi, 110–13
hunger: itinerant families, 158–60; Jamestown, Virginia, 33–35; poor populations, 213–14; post-war Europe, 166, 174–77; slave narratives, 86; wagon trains, 65, 68–69
Hungering for America: Italian, Irish, and Jewish Foodways in the Age of Migration (Diner), xix, 163
hunting practices, 4–5

ideal body type, 110–13
Illinois infantry, 92
immigrant populations: assimilation, 123, 132–35; Chinese immigrants, 62, 71–72; ethnic grocery stores, 162–63; German immigrants, 151–52; Irish immigrants, 107; Italian immigrants, 114–15, 162–63; Jewish immigrants, 116–17; late nineteenth-century era, 101–2, 107, 114–17; multiethnic dinner parties, 128–29
imperialism, 121–22
In Defense of Food: An Eater's Manifesto (Pollan), 207
indentured servants, 38–40
Indian Corn: cultivation practices, 17; good cooking skills, 131; harvest

celebration, 36; Louisiana, 13; West African diet, 27, 29
Indian Pudding, 51
indigenous foodways. *See* Amerindian food habits; immigrant populations
industrially produced food, 123–24
innovative appliances, 166, 180–81, 184–85
internment camps, 166, 172–73
Iowa, 66
Irish immigrants, 107
Iroquois, 6–8
Italian immigrants, 114–15, 162–63
itinerant families, 158–59

Jacobs, Harriet, 88–91
Jamestown, Virginia, 31–35
Japanese Americans, 166, 172–73
Jefferson, Thomas: background information, 41; conventional dining etiquette, 56–59; kitchen inventory, 54–56; request for American food, 53–54
jelly, 143
Jewish immigrants, 116–17
"John Chinaman" (song), 71–72
Johnson, Lady Bird, 200
Johnson, Lyndon B., 199
Johnson White House, 199–200
Jungle, The (Sinclair), 123, 126

Kellogg, John Harvey, xxi, 123, 124–25
Kellogg, Will Keith, 124
Kennan, George, 174
Kennedy, Jacqueline, 188, 199
Kennedy, John F., 199
Kennedy White House, 188, 199–200
Khrushchev, Nikita, 166, 184–86
King, Martin Luther, Jr., 187
Kissinger, Henry, 201
Kitchen Debate, 166, 184–86
kitchen improvements, 161–62, 166, 180–81, 184–85
kitchen inventory at Monticello, 54–56
Knight, Sarah Kemble, 46–47